The
Javanese
Family

The Javanese Family

A Study of Kinship and Socialization

HILDRED GEERTZ

WAVELAND
PRESS, INC.
Prospect Heights, Illinois

For information about this book, write or call:

Waveland Press, Inc.
P.O. Box 400
Prospect Heights, Illinois 60070
(708) 634-0081

For My Mother and Father

ACKNOWLEDGMENTS

A N anthropological research project of the kind of which my study formed a part cannot be completed without the time, effort, and material help of countless individuals and institutions. I can mention here only a few of those to whom I owe gratitude.

The greatest personal debt is to Rufus Hendon, director of our field team, and to the other members of the group: Alice Dewey, Donald Fagg, Jane Hendon, Anne Jay, Robert Jay, Anola Ryan, and Edward Ryan. Dr. Hendon read this thesis in an early form and made detailed and useful comments.

Dr. Douglas L. Oliver originated the plan of a team study of a community in Java and made all the preliminary arrangements, including going to Indonesia to lay the groundwork for our relations with the authorities there.

The grant was provided by the Ford Foundation and administered by the Center for International Studies, Massachusetts Institute of Technology. Dr. Max Millikan, director of the Center for International Studies, has been very helpful to us during all phases of the project.

The Indonesian government and the National University of Gadjah Mada in Djokjakarta, our hosts during our stay in Indonesia, were of great assistance. I wish especially to thank Mr. Suwanto, Cultural Attaché of the Indonesian Embassy at the time the original arrangements for the project were made, Professor Sardjito, President of the University of Gadjah Mada, Mr. Abdur Rachman, Secretary to the Resident of Kediri, and R. M. Soemomihardjo, the District-Officer of "Modjokuto."

The contribution made to this study by my husband, Clifford Geertz, is of course, immeasurable, and I here register only my debt for supplementary data gathered in the field, insights into Javanese culture and society, and the many critical readings he made of various drafts of this book.

Lastly, I want to thank the many Indonesians who have given of their trust and effort to this project; without their good will this study would not have been possible. To list all these friends and acquaintances in Djakarta, Djokjakarta, Kediri, and Modjokuto would be almost impossible; some of them appear in the body of this work under pseudonyms, but there are many others. I only hope that their faith in us will be justified and that this study will indeed contribute to some further understanding of the Indonesian people.

HILDRED GEERTZ

CONTENTS

ix

The
Javanese
Family

CHAPTER ONE

INTRODUCTION

1. KINSHIP IN JAVANESE SOCIETY

INDONESIA as a whole is marked by social complexity and cultural heterogeneity. Central Java,[1] that part of Indonesia which has always had the greatest economic and political development, shares in its complexity, and to a lesser extent in its heterogeneity. Its social structure is that of a modern nation, albeit a non-industrial one. Three hundred years of colonial occupation have left an imprint.

The economy is not a traditional one in any sense of the word. It is split in two, with a highly capitalized segment, oriented to production for export, and dominated by Western capital and Western management (at least at the time of study), and a poverty-stricken peasant segment, consisting largely of small holders producing commercial crops. The peasants live in large, crowded villages, which are by no means closed, self-sufficient communities. Most farmers sell a large portion of their crop at harvest, and buy much of their daily needs in markets during the rest of the year. Payment of cash wages even to fellow villagers, the existence of complex systems of credit, and the presence of Chinese and of Indonesians from other islands with very different cultural backgrounds in the town stores and markets, are further signs that economic relationships are almost

---

1. The phrase is used in the sense of the culture area of central Java, which includes the province of Central Java and most of the province of East Java.

completely modern. The political system is modern also, for there is an extensive rationalized bureaucracy, which penetrates almost all aspects of the life of a Javanese. Since the revolution of 1945-1950, a number of political innovations have been made, notably the holding of popular elections for local officials as well as national ones, and the formation of political parties, which have brought political consciousness of the most contemporary sort to the most illiterate of peasants.

The religion of Java is suitable for such a complex society. Both the Islam of the *santri* variant, and the Hindu-Buddhism of the *prijaji* variant are derived from "great traditions," that is, they are systematized, universalistic, and proselytizing. The third religious variant, the *abangan,* is a "little tradition" of animistic household and neighborhood rituals, but it too exhibits a crucial modern characteristic in that it has a tolerance for increasing secularization of many aspects of social life and for the presence of other forms of worship.

Java has had an urban civilization for at least fifteen hundred years. While the majority of the population are rice-farmers living in villages, no peasant village is far from a town, and a good many townsmen were born in villages. Urban ways of life are not foreign to any Javanese.

In this context, it is understandable that kinship, with its inflexible, particularistic, ascriptive social ties, plays only a secondary part in Javanese social structure as a whole, in contrast to the central role that kinship plays in traditional societies in structuring economic, political, and even religious behavior. That is to say, from the point of view of the functioning of the society, the Javanese kinship system, which is bilateral with the nuclear family as the most important kinship group, makes relatively few contributions.

These few contributions, however, are of utmost importance to the stability and continuity of Javanese society in its present form. They include the provision of an enduring group within which personal, economic, social and psychological needs of the members of the society are met, and within which social values are transmitted and enforced. How these two central functions are performed by the Javanese family is the major concern of this study. In particular, the second, the process of socialization—the maintenance of normative continuity from generation to generation—occupies our attention. For, as will be shown, some of the deepest and most pervasive Javanese values are maintained, not only by the socialization techniques used by Javanese adults on their children, but by the very structure of the kinship system itself.

The nuclear family, as has been stated, is the only important kinship unit. The other kinsmen are not organized into corporate groups of any sort, and serve primarily as sources of aid in trouble and of pleasurable companionship. The nuclear family is tightly knit, and, augmented occasionally by one or two relatives, it functions as an entity in regard to neighboring families and to kinsmen's families. Within a neighborhood it is the household, not its individual members, which acts on most important matters. On occasion, either the husband or wife may serve as representative of the entire household, the husband at ritual events, the wife at certain social events such as weddings and births. Each household group is seen by the members of other households as a social unit, in terms, for instance, of the borrowing and lending of labor, the attribution of general social status, and general social participation. Economically, the nuclear family household is the basic consumption group. While each member —even the children—retains title on his own property, any goods which enter the household are usually redistributed among the members according to need. However, the household is rarely a complete unit for production; this is true even for farmers, because rice-agriculture necessarily involves the labor of a larger number of people than a household alone can provide. Land is individually owned or controlled; a man's kinsmen other than his primary relatives have little more claim to the use of that land or to the work on the land than do his neighbors. Townsmen have even fewer economic ties to their kinsmen than do farmers, for they work as individuals, usually either for the civil bureaucracy or in trade. Even those townsmen who are self-employed, as for instance a man with a small cigarette factory, do not organize their enterprise in the form of a family business but employ outsiders just as frequently as family members.

In addition to ritual and economic functions, and the social-ization of children, the nuclear family household performs a further function. This is the provision for those family members who cannot support themselves—the sick, the unemployed, the aged, the parentless child. All of these are absorbed into the families of their close kinsmen and given the care they need. This social security aspect of the family is significant for the func-tioning of Javanese society as a whole. It provides a measure of adaptability and flexibility to the society, since it allows free movement in and out of the labor pool without strain on the other institutions of the society. However, the amount of actual aid given relatives outside the nuclear family should not be over-emphasized. While any kinsman has a moral claim to be helped in time of trouble, the strength of the claim diminishes rapidly with the distance of relationship.

To a Javanese, kinship is only one element among many—such as status, age, and wealth—which define the relationship between man and man. In fact, the most significant character-istic of the Javanese view of kin ties is the amount of freedom of action it permits the individual. In any given social situation, kinship is only one factor among many others which may influ-ence the behavior of the individual. If, for instance, there is an awkward wealth differential between two kinsmen, or a person-ality conflict between them, or geographic distance due to occu-pational contingencies, they can ignore the kinship ties or accentuate them as they wish in keeping with the pressures of their particular situation.

The manipulability of kin ties in practice is related to the nature of the kinship system itself—its minimizing of differentia-tion, the absence of kin-based social groups, and, further, the weakness, vagueness, and limited number of its jural norms, the duties and rights between kin. Even between parents and chil-dren, kinship obligations and rights are given a fairly wide lati-tude of individual interpretation. Property transfers at divorce and death are usually settled, not so much with reference to abstract legalistic rules, but in accordance with the specific situa-tion and with a more substantive equity which takes into account the needs of the individuals involved. There is no preferential

marriage pattern; selection of mate is the concern of the individual and his immediate family. What I have called "manipulability of kin ties" means not so much an active switching and
realigning of kin categories by the individual to suit his own
purposes as a lack of coerciveness in the kin categories themselves, a tolerance which makes it easier to evade kin responsibilities and which narrows the range of effective kinship.

A Javanese sees each relative as a unique individual. How he
will behave toward this relative is a function of at least six different factors: sex, relative age, class position, religio-ideological
views, personal feelings, and kinship. Outside the circle of primary relatives the kinship element is often the weakest of the six
factors.

Nevertheless, for each Javanese, his family—his parents, his
children, and, usually, his spouse—are the most important people
in the world. They give him emotional security and provide a
stable point of social orientation. They give him moral guidance,
helping him from infancy through old age to learn, and relearn,
the values of Javanese culture. The process of socialization is a
continuous one throughout the life of the individual; and it is
a man's closest relatives who, by their day-to-day comment, both
verbal and non-verbal, keep him from deviating too far from the
cultural norms.

2. THE SETTING

Modjokuto,[2] the town in which this study was undertaken,
lies within the culture-area of central Java, but at its eastern edge
and some distance from the influence of the courts of Djokjakarta and Surakarta. It has a population of about 20,000 people
and serves as a commercial, governmental, and educational center
for an area of about 75 square miles (the District of Modjokuto).
The town is located on the edge of a rice plain, next to gradually rising uplands which before the war held a number of Dutch

---

2. "Modjokuto" is a pseudonym as are all names of Javanese persons
ing in these pages.

plantations growing coffee, tea, and rubber. In the plains near the town, there were extensive Dutch sugar enterprises, remnants of which still survive today, though operating on a much reduced scale. Even during the period of intensive Dutch economic activity (which had begun to decline in the area by the beginning of the 1930's), there were few Dutch people who lived in the town of Modjokuto, and these had little personal contact with its inhabitants; but the impact of Dutch enterprises on the economic system itself was, of course, great.

Modjokuto is located at the fork of three roads. One leads to the south and east through the highlands. One leads west about fifteen miles to the city of Bragang on the Brantas River, where the ancient Hindu-Javanese kingdom of Bragang had its capital in the thirteenth century. Stone temples covered with carvings are scattered throughout the valley, at two of which, close to Modjokuto, offerings are sometimes left by the local people for the spirits that still inhabit them. Bragang now is a sleepy city. It is several times the size of Modjokuto and is the administrative center for the greater part of the Brantas valley, of which Modjokuto forms one District.

The third road goes north to another town about fifteen miles away, which is also on the Brantas River. Formerly a center for river traffic, and an important shipping point for the sugar produced in the area, this town today is still a lively commercial center, with an important main railway running through it which connects the huge port city of Surabaya at the mouth of the Brantas with the inland court cities of the central rice plain, Djokja and Solo.

In addition to the roads which join Modjokuto to the outside world, there is a narrow-gauge railroad which comes in from Bragang, turns a sharp right angle at the center of Modjokuto, and goes on to the next town north with six trains daily in each direction. The trains, formerly loaded with shipments of sugar cane, are now busy taking the numerous market peddlers of Modjokuto on daily trips in and out of the surrounding villages, towns, and cities. The roads are heavily used, with buses and jitneys carrying as many people as the railroad does, heavy trucks transporting Modjokuto's surplus cash crops out to the port of Surabaya, and ox carts, horse carts, bicycles, and heavily loaded pedestrians constantly moving goods between villages and towns.

The three roads out of Modjokuto fork under a huge banyan tree, underneath which is a small stone statue of the Hindu elephant god, Ganesha, which is not worshipped as that god but considered the dwelling place of a powerful spirit that can aid one in the face of sickness and poverty. Across the street from the banyan tree is a large Western style house where, until 1941, the Dutch Controller, the administrative official at the District level lived. Today it is a government hospital. On the town square behind the banyan tree are the ruins of five or six Western style houses where the offices of the railroad were until their destruction in the revolution in 1950.

On the third corner of the crossroads, set in behind a large open area and minor buildings, is the residence and office of the District Head of Modjokuto, the *Wedono*.[3] The greater portion of this building is the *pendapa*, a kind of oversized summerhouse about a hundred feet square and always cool, dark, and dignified looking. Here the District Head meets his official guests, performs his business, and has official celebrations. At one side is a small house where his office staff have their desks. The District of Modjokuto is divided into five Subdistricts. One of these Subdistricts also has its administrative center in the town of Modjokuto, and the office and residence of the Head of the Subdistrict of Modjokuto are nearby.

District and Subdistrict represent rather arbitrary administrative units, artificial segments of the rice plain with its crisscross of roads and villages and small towns, cut up for easy handling in the tax books and other official records. The town of Modjokuto is not a political entity, for the next administrative units under the Subdistrict are its component villages. The

---

3. The spelling of Indonesian words conforms to the current official orthography. Javanese words are spelled in accordance with the system currently employed by Balai Pustaka (a publishing agency of the Ministry of Education) in its publications in that language. This is identical with the orthography of Th. Pigeaud's Javaans-Nederlands Handwoordenboek (Groningen, n.d.), except that *oe* is replaced by *u*. Arabic words are also spelled in accordance with the Javanese system.

town of Modjokuto is made up of the village of Modjokuto plus considerable portions of three neighboring villages. Modjokuto is an overgrown village, once swollen by the Dutch enterprises which had some of their offices and residences in the town and owing its present size to the presence of the government offices and the market.

The nearest thing to a natural social unit, or community, within which the members carry on the majority of their activities is the Subdistrict. Most Javanese, even the simplest peasants, have a wider social horizon than their own neighborhood or even their own village. Not only do trade and governmental affairs extend over long distances, but also family members are often scattered over a number of villages in the area. Most of the traffic goes in and out of the town, which is a commercial center for a wide area that coincides approximately with the officially delimited Modjokuto Subdistrict. With the exception of certain urban occupational groups and perhaps the inhabitants of some of the peripheral villages, most members of the Subdistrict carry on the larger portion of their activities within its borders, the village of Modjokuto together with the seventeen villages that surround it, an area of about thirty square miles with a population of about 87,000 people.

Governmental agencies which employ townspeople and bring village people into town include the police, the irrigation service, the agricultural extension service, the government pawnshop, the government salt monopoly, the hospital, the religious office where marriages and divorces are handled, and, more and more, the schools. Modjokuto has twelve public elementary schools, about five private ones and two public and four private secondary schools (offering a total of ten years of school). Villages usually have elementary schools but have to send their children to town for further education. Townspeople often try to send their children to the secondary schools in the larger cities, where they are thought to get a better education.

One focus of activity of the town is the government, the other the market. Commerce in Modjokuto is roughly of two main sorts. The first has to do with major transfers of goods in and out of Modjokuto toward the port of Surabaya, the buying up in quantity of cash crops for speculation or export, and the bringing in of goods manufactured overseas (dishes, flashlights, cloth). The other is comprised of small-scale transactions on a local level. The first is dominated mainly by Chinese, of whom there are about 1800 in the town. The second, the selling of daily food needs to townsmen, the buying up of small quantities of cash crops to sell to Chinese wholesalers, and the retail sale of cheap manufactured goods obtained from Chinese merchants, is mainly in the hands of Javanese and a few Arabs. The Chinese operate from stores and warehouses on the main streets of Modjokuto; the Javanese trade centers on the two town market places, but is actually a great network of tiny transactions spreading over the entire countryside, with larger knots in centers like Modjokuto. Several of the minor towns in the Modjokuto District also have markets, and some professional Javanese market peddlers divide their activities among several places. Since trade in rice is controlled by the government in order to keep the price stable, most of the commercial rice goes through government channels (although the handling of it is contracted by large Chinese firms). Other crops that move in and out of the town in quantity are onions, corn, soybeans, and peanuts.

The social organization of the Javanese side of the market complex is complicated. Although Javanese tradesmen are rugged individualists and the market as a whole seems to operate along classic Adam Smith lines of supply-demand dynamics, the number of people involved in a presumably simple movement of goods from producer to consumer is enormous. Rapid turnover of small quantities of goods, tiny profit levels, and a minute division of labor mean that everyone in the market gets a small profit and that, by and large, no one becomes rich. There are two or three Javanese store owners competing with the Chinese in their own sphere, and about half a dozen large-scale Javanese dealers in *batik* cloth (which, although ultimately tied to the Chinese import of muslin, is manufactured mainly by Javanese in the big cities) who are quite wealthy by local standards. Almost all townsmen have tried their hand at marketing (including a surprising proportion of the government employees), especially during the periods of inflation in the Japanese occupation and the postwar period; most, however, feel that it is a job for professionals and that amateurs are apt to lose their money.

Industry in Modjokuto is confined to a few small firms: a Chinese-owned soft drink factory, a Madurese-owned cigarette factory, several Javanese-owned firms making cigarettes, hats, soybean cake, cheap work clothes, and a few others. Two Javanese who had formerly been government officials and who had secured government loans started large-scale firms after the revolution, one a combination rice and sugar mill, the other a lumber firm making cheap boxes for a Dutch beer company in Surabaya. There are also a number of bicycle and automobile repair shops of both the small-scale Javanese-run and larger Chinese-run varieties.

The town also has a variety of commercial entertainment facilities. There is a Chinese-owned movie house where Malayan, Philippine, Indonesian, Indian, Chinese and American films of the cowboy and Tarzan type are shown every night. There is another theater also owned by a Chinese, where Javanese troupes perform plays and "operas" (*sandiwara*, *ludrug*, and *wayang wong*). There is a recognized vice district. A number of traveling troupes of singers, dancers, and players who come into Modjokuto occasionally either play from door to door or can be hired to put on a regular performance.

The occupational structure of Modjokuto includes many kinds of work. In the villages nearly everyone is a farmer, even the village headman and his staff (although they may have most of the manual work done for them). Some village men are also buyers of crops for resale and may even do this full time, but other than these and an occasional carpenter, bricklayer, or entertainer there are not many specialists in the villages. Townsmen, although they may own land, rarely work it themselves. They may be government clerks, policemen, teachers, tailors, food sellers, cigarette stand keepers, coffee-shop owners, cloth salesmen, railroad men, crop speculators, jitney drivers, labor union leaders, professional dancers, doctors, or curers. The largest number of townsmen are unskilled laborers who are underemployed for the most part and who eke out a living doing odd carrying jobs around the market or seasonal farm labor, once in a while attempting a minor market transaction on borrowed capital. Some of these people formerly worked in Dutch households and a few now work in the Dutch private hospital which serves the estate employees of firms some distance away. Some work for Chinese, some in the houses of more well-to-do Javanese.

The government employees are the elite of Modjokuto society. They occupy the attractive brick houses on the main streets and maintain a style of living, usually beyond their limited means, which includes a refined round of social calls, weddings, and circumcisions, certain Westernized standards of food and entertainment, high education for their children, through college if possible, and a great proliferation of clubs and organizations. It was in this educated segment—and that of the prosperous traders—that the Javanese nationalist movement arose.

In addition to political parties, which themselves involve a subsidiary proliferation of committees, women's auxiliaries, and the like, the Modjokuto elite have many other kinds of organizations: private school boosters (the most private one having a special cemetery for its members), saving societies, tennis clubs, boy and girl scouts, student clubs, special occupation groups such as policemen's or pawn-office employees' societies, women's clubs, *ad hoc* committees for the celebration of national holidays, and mystical study societies.

These last are the religious organizations characteristic of the government employees, small groups of "students" who gather together, usually around a respected "teacher" who may have learned his lore from another "teacher" in a court city in central Java, and strive together to achieve a kind of cognitive mystic understanding of the god within themselves. This particular variant of Javanese religion, the *prijaji* variant, is highly influenced by Hindu-Buddhist doctrines. Just as the government-employee-centered political organizations penetrate, to some extent, down to other occupational groups oriented around the market, so also do the religious movements or sects sometimes have followers in non-governmental circles. And, just as the political organizations, as they move downward in the society from the most Westernized (superficially, at least) segment to the more traditional segments, become less Westernized and more concerned with religious elements (as opposed to ideological ones), so also do the religious sects become reinterpreted and tend to lose their intellectualistic flavor, becoming more and more like curing societies.

Below the bureaucratic elite come the prosperous traders, some of the wealthier of whom (those who deal in fine Djokja *batik* cloth in particular) pattern their style of living after that of the government employees, with whom they mix socially to some extent, join their mystical religious group on occasion, and try to educate their children to move into that admired class. It is among the next lower group, the successful traders, the Javanese shopkeepers, tailors, owners of small cigarette factories, and the like, that Islam is strongest. These, the *santris*, are the people who attend the big mosque near the market on Fridays, who piously pray five times a day, unlike the majority of Javanese, and who form the core of the Islamic political parties. The Islamic community itself is split into a modernist and a conservative faction. The modernist is more completely town-based; its leadership comes from the educated children of the prosperous tradesmen and is characterized by a revisionist, "protestant-type" theology and a rationalistic social reform movement. In Modjokuto that movement is centered in a highly active but small core of people who run the Masjumi political party and the local chapter of Muhammadijah, a non-political social service organization which has an orphanage, a school that goes through ten grades, and religious study groups. The conservative faction of the Islamic community is village-based. The leaders (except for a few townsmen) are old-fashioned Koranic teachers, representatives of the pre-twentieth century fusion of Islam and the peasant tradition *(abangan)* of curing and protection against evil spirits, who have schools in village areas for teaching young men the chanting of the Koran. The conservative Moslems are represented by the political party of Nahadatul Ulama, the Moslem Teachers Union.

Below the two upper classes in the town, the government workers and the prosperous tradesmen, comes the great mass of townsmen who live in small houses in the interior of the city blocks: the small peddlers, the cheap artisans, the load-bearers, and the unemployed. Oriented more toward the villages than the upper classes, and often still having family connections in the villages, these people have a religious outlook similar to that of the peasants. Without the consciousness of in-group and the tendency to form organizations, which are characteristic of the bureaucratic elite, and without the feeling of community, centering on the mosque and the political party, which is characteristic of the Moslems, these town-dwelling peasants have a strong individualism and a tough-minded empiricism about religion. They believe that the purpose of religion is to protect one and one's immediate family from poverty and sickness. The central ritual is a family meal (the *slametan*), to which the men of the houses in the immediate neighborhood are invited, at which Arabic prayers are chanted by those few who know them and at which an assortment of Hindu-Buddhist deities, Allah, Muhammed, and Fatimah, the guardian spirit of the village, and a host of nameless spirits located variously in roof eaves, wells, the hearth, and so on are called on for their protection, good will, or non-interference. The chanting of spells (whether for the *slametan* or for curing or for weaning a baby) is the essential element in the peasant religion, together with certain ritual actions such as the burning of incense and the serving of appropriate foods.

There are other segments of the Modjokuto population that are not so easily classified. The railroad employees at the administrative level are among the bureaucratic elite. Most of the railroad workers are closer to the peasants and, with the plantation workers, who are largely situated outside the bounds of Modjokuto Subdistrict, form the local center for leftist trade-unionism. (Other elements in the union movement are certain teachers' unions and an organization of peasants, primarily those who have seized portions of the Dutch plantation land, who are endeavoring to keep their squatter's rights.) There are small groups of Christians, whose churches are often dominated by Chinese. One such group, which is almost entirely Javanese and belongs to the Dutch Reformed Church, is made up wholly of employees of the Dutch hospital, who have a style of life similar to that of the town government employees. Another rather large segment of the town population is made up of the high school students, who range in age from thirteen to twenty-five and many of whom are from village homes, living in town at the homes of relatives or boarding singly or in groups at various private homes. They are more Westernized than their parents, ardently nationalistic, divided into various political factions (although many attempt to be apolitical) and are preparing themselves for careers in the bureaucracy. Of the six secondary schools in Modjokuto, there is only one which purports to teach technical subjects such as automobile repair and carpentry, but many of its graduates, too aspire to the civil service.

The town of Modjokuto is fairly typical of central Javanese towns. Although no two Javanese towns are exactly alike sociologically, Modjokuto is not specialized in any particular direction: almost all the important aspects of Javanese society and culture are well represented.

CHAPTER TWO

THE STRUCTURE OF THE
JAVANESE KINSHIP SYSTEM

1. KINSHIP TERMINOLOGY

The Fundamental Pattern

WE BEGIN our description of the Javanese kinship system with an analysis of the kinship terminology, for the terms that a people employ to discriminate among their relatives make up a coherent system, a basic relational pattern which underlies their particular view of kinship. The aspects of kin relationships emphasized by kinship terminology may not necessarily be the most important ones in terms of actual kinship behavior, but they are always of some significance.

The basic form of the Javanese terminological system is bilateral and generational. That is, the kin terms are the same whether the linking relative is the mother or the father, and all the members of each generation are grouped verbally. All the members of one's own generation, i.e., one's siblings and cousins, are called by the same or similar terms; all the members of one's parents' generation, i.e. parents, their siblings and their cousins, are called by another set of similar terms; all the members of the grandparental generation, including the siblings of grandparents are identified by a single term; and so on. The result is a horizontal stratification of all relatives: each Javanese sees himself in the center of an array of "grandparents," "parents," "siblings," "children," and "grandchildren."[1]

Two other distinctions complete the analysis of this rather simple relational pattern: the distinction of seniority and the distinction of sex. The distinction of seniority serves to subdivide the generational categories into junior and senior sections. Within one's own sibling group, this criterion marks off one's younger siblings from one's older siblings. One's parent's siblings are distinguished according to whether they are older or younger than one's parents. For cousins, the referent point for the criterion of seniority is not age relative to Ego, but the relative age of the two siblings who are the connecting links between the two cousins (i.e., Ego's and the cousin's parents or their respective grandparents). Table I indicates the seniority-juniority distinction. Note that the seniority principle is applied only to those kin who fall in one's own generation and that of one's parents, and that all "grandparents" have equal status (although their descendants do not) as do all "children."

The fourth principle is that of sex of the occupant of the kin position. If the person in the parental generation is a woman, she is a *bu*; if a man, he is a *pak*. If the senior sibling is a woman, she is a *mbakju*; and if a man, he is a *mas*. The criterion of sex, like the criterion of seniority, does not apply to generations above the parents or below Ego; if it is necessary, a descriptive word meaning "male" or "female" can be added—for instance, "younger sibling" is *adik*, while "female younger sibling" is *adik wédok*.

These four principles for differentiating and equating various kinsmen—bilaterality, generation, seniority and sex—are all that are necessary to account for the pattern of kin terminology (see

---

1. The system of cousin terminology may be considered either Hawaiian or Eskimo, depending on whether the classification is limited to certain distinctive terms of reference or whether the terms of address (which are also used as nouns for reference) are to be considered. Some terms of reference for cousins *(misanan, nak-sanak, mindoan)* are never applied to siblings, and one phrase *(sedulur tjer* "real sibling") is only used to refer to siblings. However, cousins are also frequently referred to by the same terms as siblings *(sedulur, mas, mbakju, adik)*. Cousins are always addressed in the same way as siblings. For this reason, Hawaiian is the preferable classification. See Appendix I for a detailed list of all kinship terms.

Table I) and, in fact, are also significant underlying assumptions of the more general kinship system. However, there is another principle, almost ignored in the kin terminology, which operates to distinguish between functioning social groups of kin and which is perhaps more important in the definition of a man's

Table I
Schematic Diagram of the System of Javanese Kin Terms, Showing How the Principles of Generation and Seniority Combine to Form a Layered Ranking of Kinsmen.

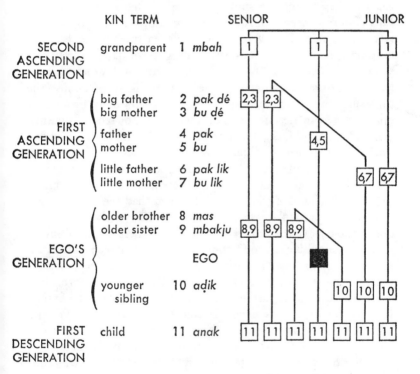

In this chart, □ represents a kinsman of either sex, a vertical line represents descent, and a horizontal or diagonal line connects siblings. "Senior" and "junior" refer to age relationships within these groups of siblings.

relationships to his various kin (his duties and rights in regard to them) than these, and that is distance.

In keeping with the functional importance of the nuclear family, some (albeit slight) distinction is made between the nuclear family and other relatives. The suffixes *ḍé* (big) or *lik* (little) which serve to indicate relative seniority among parent's siblings, also indicate that they are not the actual parents. But for kinsmen extending away outside the nuclear family's borders, there is no way of suggesting that some are nearer than others. And in actual practice, in daily talk, even the distinction between nuclear and non-nuclear family is ignored; cousins are always addressed in exactly the same manner as siblings; uncles and aunts may be addressed as simply "father" and "mother"; and nephews, grandnephews, etc., are spoken to in the same manner as one's own children. Even affinal relatives are addressed and frequently referred to as if they were blood kin, even though the Javanese have special terms for son-in-law, daughter-in-law, brother- or sister-in-law, and parents-in-law. If one asks a Javanese his relationship to a particular man, he is more likely to choose the term suggestive of close relationship ("Why, he's my brother!") than a more precise one (e.g., brother-in-law, or second cousin).

This failure of the kin terminology system to sharply distinguish categories of distance is not a reflection of an actual social situation of close affiliation among a widespread kin group. The real situation is one of strong differentiation of nuclear family, near kin, and distant kin. The fact that the terminology ignores this particular aspect of social reality derives from the deep-rooted Javanese conviction that it is best to avoid or to play down divisive or conflicting tendencies between individuals in the hope that by verbally ignoring them social relationships will flow more smoothly. Thus it is usually in just those relationships where there is the most strain that it is hardest to extract from an informant a correct statement of relationship. Women who have brought up some other woman's child will usually claim the child to be their own; parents-in-law similarly are careful not to discriminate verbally between their own child and the child's spouse.

Social Relationships: Respect and Familiarity

If the kinship terminology sorts out relatives into generations and senior-vs.-junior subdivisions of the generations, is this sorting of any social structural significance? Is it simply an arbitrary labeling, or does it refer to some socially functional grouping of relatives? I have already noted that the most important dimension of grouping of relatives is their nearness to Ego, and that this criterion of grouping is not evident in the kinship terminology. If the kin terms do not indicate institutionalized social groups and on the other hand are not simply arbitrary labels, a third possibility exists: that they indicate some specific social relationships between Ego and each relative. In considering this last possibility, I offer the hypothesis that the most important of these specific social relationships connoted by the kin terms used between any dyad of relatives is that of respect vs. familiarity.

Respect, *urmat*, or *adji*, is an element of every social situation in Java. Perhaps the first thought a Javanese has when he meets a new person is "What degree of respect should I show him?" To address a person with respect does not necessarily mean to be subservient to his authority or even to admit to having less prestige than he. It is primarily a matter of etiquette, the rules of proper behavior in specific situations. The expression of respect places the two people in a known position in regard to one another so that further interaction can take place in a controlled and orderly way and uncertainties of expectation will be minimized.

What position the two people take depends on a number of distinct ranking systems which are independent and which may conflict with or reinforce each other; that is, an individual may be high on one rank ladder and low on another. These systems include sex, relative age, wealth, occupation, and style of life (which is closely related to occupation and refers to a ranging of people along a continuum with those nearest to the *prijaji* way of life at the top). A second determinant of the respect position that two people will take toward each other is distance. One ought to speak with respect to any unfamiliar person, not only out of care not to offend, but also because respect in itself is also an expression of distance and, thus, one further specification of the relationship between the two people. For instance, if a man and a woman meet, all other things being equal, the man should receive respect from the woman and not give as much respect to her; but if she is a woman with whom he is not on familiar terms or should not be (e.g., if she is married), he should speak respectfully to her. If she is of *prijaji* background, or if he is a peasant, she will speak to him without respect, all the more so if she is acquainted with him, and he will respond with expressions of the highest respect.

Respect is shown in several ways: by posture, gestures and tone of voice, term of address, and, above all, by the language-level spoken. It is impossible for two people to meet and to speak Javanese together without precisely specifying their respect relationship to one another; such specifications are inherent in the structure of the Javanese language, just as the indication of time —past, present, or future—is inherent in the English language. How exact and unavoidable these indications of status are must be experienced to be appreciated. There are two major levels of language, respect *(krama)* and familiarity *(ngoko)*. These in turn can be modulated to add two more levels, high respect *(krama inggil)* and respectful familiarity *(ngoko madya)*, by substituting within the basic matrix of respect or familiarity high-flown words and phrases and honorific pronouns. (There is a third level of language, roughly between *ngoko* and *krama*, called *krama madya*—"middle" *krama*—which is the variant of *krama* spoken by peasants and lower class urban people, the majority of the population perhaps, but which is functionally equivalent to *krama* in the following discussions).

In the wider world of non-kin, friends who are precisely the same in age, sex, wealth, and so on may address each other with exactly the same degree of respect or familiarity. But among kin there can be no such equal relationships. There is no one among all his kin who is precisely equal to Ego; even his brothers are divided into those above him and those below him. All kin above Ego (not in the sense of older than he, but of senior in position) must be addressed with respectful language of some degree. How the various layers of the kin term system coincide with linguistic respect distinctions is shown in Table II.

As can be seen from the diagram, all kin whom Ego calls "grandparent" should be addressed in linguistic forms of high respect. All kin whom Ego calls "mother" or "father" should be

Table II
Schematic Diagram of System of Javanese Kin Terms, Showing How Kin Term Ranking Interlocks with Linguistic Etiquette System of Respect-Familiarity.

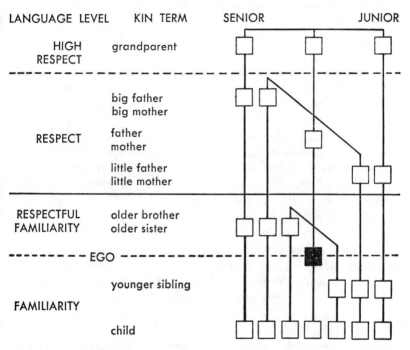

LANGUAGE LEVEL	KIN TERM	SENIOR		JUNIOR
HIGH RESPECT	grandparent			
RESPECT	big father / big mother			
	father / mother			
	little father / little mother			
RESPECTFUL FAMILIARITY	older brother / older sister			
EGO				
FAMILIARITY	younger sibling			
	child			

addressed with linguistic respect. Those in Ego's own generation and below can be addressed with familiarity, but those he calls "older brother" or "older sister" should be given some indication of their superior status.

Their superior status, however, does not necessarily carry with it any power. It is not accompanied by special rights of any kind, whether of inheritance or of authority (outside of the nuclear family), or any ritual or economic privileges, but is simply a fact of seniority to be recognized in etiquette. Nevertheless, it is an important aspect of the relationship a Javanese has with every kinsman and is a part of his attitude toward each of them. To speak on the language level of respect is not considered "natural" or "comfortable"; a child speaks the language of familiarity with his mother and siblings, at least until he is ten or twelve, and gradually is taught to shift away from this direct informal speech to a more modulated and polite manner. (Most people continue to speak to the mother in the same way as they did as children; a few shift to respect in adulthood.) The language of respect is thought to be hard to speak because of the social tensions inherent in the situation; it is referred to usually as "language" (*basa*) while the speech of familiarity has no special label, is thought of simply as "ordinary" (*bijasa*) or "comfortable" (*kepénak*) talk. Even to make the first smallest shift to respectful familiarity means to hold in check natural impulses to casual speech, to avoid or carefully select pronouns, and, among some groups, to substitute high-flown terms for words that refer to the body, behavior, or belongings of the person spoken to.

To make the next shift, to the language of respect, requires an even more artificial kind of speech. Even though respect is "difficult," every Javanese has learned the skill of shifting language levels by the time he is adult; but the feeling of constraint is still there. Many young students never write letters to their parents for fear of making an error, more obvious because in writing; they communicate, if at all, to a younger sibling in familiar language messages to be relayed to the parents.

There are class differences in the style with which the categories of high respect, respect, and respectful familiarity are filled. Among the minority of upper aristocrats and office workers (*prijajis*) in Modjokuto, grandparents, sometimes uncles and aunts, and all above are addressed in highly refined language (*krama inggil*), and in general the status differences among the kin are highly accentuated. On the other hand, many "average men" speak to their grandparents in almost the same manner as to their parents, with only subtle indications of the high respect category. Some Javanese use the familiar language extensively, muting down the differences between the status levels, speaking to parents and parents' siblings almost the same as to own older sibling but adding minor suggestions of respect. No matter in what style the categories are filled, however, the over-all pattern of generational differences remains.

Conflict between Respect Systems

The over-all pattern of generational differentiation is only one of several culture patterns which guide an individual in his relations to kinsmen. Its coerciveness is limited, and—in the face of contradictions between prescribed respect behavior to a kinsman and his position on respect scales other than kinship, such as class—it may give way. For instance, an informant whose family were moderately well-off peasants in a village near Modjokuto had an aunt who, after several marriages, had finally married a government employee who had risen high in the bureaucracy and had adopted the style of life of the *prijaji*. This informant addressed her aunt in highly refined language far different from that which she used in speaking to the most respected of her other kin.

Conflict between respect systems is common. For example, a twelve-year-old boy protested to his mother against having to address his two-year-old "grandparent" in the appropriate terms of the relationship. The mother said, "But he's your grandparent," and compromised, allowing her son to use familiar language to the child, as was suitable to his age, but with high pronouns and continued use of the term of address *mbah*, with the addition of *lik*, thus "little grandparent." A third example of how the kinship terms and respect levels can be shifted (with always a consciousness of shift *away* from an established pattern) is that of a twenty-year-old informant who had a thirty-five-year-old nephew. She should have called him "child" and been addressed by him as "mother," but they both felt awkward doing this and shifted to "younger sibling" and "older sister."

An exception often made to the pattern of respect to kinsmen is in the relationship between grandchild and own grandparent. When, as is often the case in Java, grandparent and grandchild are linked closely by mutual affection, the child will speak familiarly to the grandparent long after he has adopted respect language in addressing his own parents. However, when he is fully adult, the grandchild is likely, finally, to change to some version of high respect.

The more distant the relationship, the more likely it is that, in the event of any contradiction between respect standards, the kinship criteria will give way. Thus, although the structure of the terminological system may not indicate closeness or distance of relationship, the manner in which the system is employed may. Outside the circle of close relatives, kinship itself is no longer the primary determinant of the kin term and style of speech; other factors, such as age or class status, may be of greater influence.

Kinship Terms and Non-Kinsmen

Kin terms are used to address all persons, kin and non-kin, with the exception of one's own servants and kin who are younger than or junior to the speaker. To address a person without using such a term (and there is a specific word for "to address by name only": *ndjangkar*) either with or without his name indicates disrespect and extreme familiarity. Even children of neighbors are addressed with a modifying term, "child" (*nak*), before their name. The ranking within the kin terms themselves adds an extra fillip of specificity in addressing a non-kin. If it is desired to show high respect, the term "big father" (*pak ḍé*) can be used; if respect plus a little warmth, "little father" (*pak lik*) is appropriate. "Grandparent," except where the person is quite old, does not suggest even greater respect. "Big father" (*pak ḍé*) connotes about the highest respect for a middle-aged person which such kin terms can show; to go further, aristocratic titles (i.e., *dèn, ndara*) are employed. (There is an attempt today to eliminate this usage as undemocratic; and most dignitaries are addressed as *bapak*, "father," or *ibu*, "mother," or various Indonesian terms, such as *tuan*, "sir," *njonja*, "madam," and *saudara*, "kinsman," are used.)

2. THE KINDRED AND AFFINAL RELATIVES

Extent and Cohesiveness of the Kindred

The Javanese have no concept of the kindred[2] as a unit, and no word for it. What words there are (*kulawarga, sanak-sedulur*,

---

2. I use "kindred" here in the sense that G. P. Murdock uses it: the consanguineal kin group which consists of one's "own nearest genealogical kins-

sedulur) mean simply "relatives." These "relatives" may be widely scattered socially and geographically or they may form a tightly knit group, depending on the particular circumstances of each family. From the point of view of the individual, there is a pool of relatives, a series of vaguely defined circles of kin outside the nuclear family which fades gradually into the general society of non-kin, each such series of circles being slightly different for each individual. This pool of relatives can be drawn on for assistance at various stages in one's life, the degree of distance being the measure of the strength of one's claim.

The limits of spread of kinship are indefinite, but the Javanese make some distinction between "near kin" (*sedulur tjedak*) "distant kin" (*sedulur adoh*). The first group are, usually, one's four grandparents and their descendants, that is, one's uncles, aunts, and grandparents (the immediate family of one's own parents), their children and grandchildren, and one's own children and grandchildren—with the possible addition of one's great-grandparents, and great-grandchildren. It is this group, the near kin, who for the present purposes can be considered the kindred. The boundaries are fluid in practice. A close relative may become, in effect, distant as a result of a quarrel, geographic distance, or his moving into another class; one who is distant kin may, through prolonged geographical proximity, or by joining the household, develop a more intense personal relationship with a group of his distant kin and come to be considered one of the family.

The same sort of situational considerations which govern the limits of the kindred also determine how cohesive it will be. Firmly entrenched peasant families with sufficient landholdings may maintain close relationships with a wide number of kinsmen. For instance, a group of related village headmen and lesser officials in a cluster of neighboring villages who maintain a tradition of holding such offices going back several generations may keep a history of their own genealogy, and, by means of strategically

men irrespective of through which parent they are related to" one (*Social Structure*, New York, 1949, p. 44). "In our own society, where its members are collectively called 'kinfolk' or 'relatives' it includes that group of kinsmen who may be expected to be present and participant on important ceremonial occasions, such as weddings, christenings, funerals, Thanksgiving and Christmas dinners, and 'family reunions'." (pp. 56-57).

placed endogamous marriages, constantly reinforce their strong kin organization. In most cases, however, the small size of the portions of land and the practice of equal inheritance among siblings diffuses the property, making it necessary for at least some of the relatives to leave the village or town of their origin to look for a living elsewhere. In addition, there is a marked tendency to marry women from other villages or towns and to move to the wife's village. Consequently, the members of the kindred of most Javanese—particularly the poorer landless peasants and townsmen—are scattered, rather than united in one place.

Rights and Duties of Kinsmen

The obligations and rights among members of the kindred are limited. Members are expected to help with such festivities as weddings, circumcisions, and births by contributing substantially in food, money, and labor. A kin group which is cohesive can marshal a large quantity of goods and facilities among themselves for these occasions, a fact which adds further to their actual wealth and prestige. Distant kin are expected to attend such affairs if they live nearby, but they do not have to contribute more than a friend or neighbor would.

These festivities require women's work more than men's, and consequently bring together the women of a family more often than the men. Further, women appear to be more eager to aid their female rather than their male relatives. Thus, the work of these celebrations is usually carried out largely by the kinswomen of the wife of the household. In general, too, women maintain closer ties with their kindred than men do. After marriage, and moving away, daughters usually keep close relationships with their parental families than sons do, and adult sisters —and their respective daughters—keep in closer touch with each other than they do with their brothers, or than brothers do.

There is a moral obligation to care for any close kinsman who is needy. This particularly applies to one's own parents and siblings, but it may also apply to secondary kin such as a destitute aunt or a nephew if there is no one closer to take care of them. Kin who have are obliged to help kin who have not, the only questions of obligation which may be raised being the actual degree of need of the one kinsman and the actual wealth of the other. This does not by any means imply that all property is shared by all; each kinsman is expected to support himself, and there are restraining factors to keep a man from asking for help. He may be proud. He may fear refusal by his relative's spouse, who, unsympathetic, will usually want to give little or nothing to the needy one. A traveling family member, even though distantly related must always be given lodging if he asks for it.

A person who cannot support himself, or one who has no spouse to live with, may come to live permanently in a kinsman's household, the home of one's own children being most preferred. With the exception of grandparents' siblings, who sometimes, in their old age, become dependent on the children of their nieces and nephews, members of the circle of distant kin rarely enter into so close an arrangement. In contrast, any of those who are in the category of near kin may be found as peripheral members of Javanese households.

Affinal Relatives

There are many reasons for the strong tendency for Javanese to limit the occupancy in a household to members of the nuclear family, one of the most important being the psychological tension between affinal relatives. The Javanese feel that affinals are, in a sense, kinsmen—and yet that they are not; and the tensions center on this contradiction. It is interesting that the modes of address, in Javanese always a sensitive indicator of nuances of relationship, are always tipped toward the respectful side between affinal relatives. Brothers- and sisters-in-law are nearly always (always, if of opposite sex) addressed in the language of respect. Even a daughter-in-law, although technically a "child" and therefore to be addressed in familiar language, is usually addressed in terms with at least some subtle respect indications.

The son- and daughter-in-law, on the other hand, should always be extremely respectful to the parent-in-law. Since most kinship responsibilities fall on the woman, a daughter-in-law, if she lives nearby, is expected to send a fairly steady stream of little gifts to her mother-in-law; and the mother-in-law, if she is better off, sends presents in return, usually for the grandchildren.

One informant, Juminah, furnished an illustration of this when she described her duties to her parents-in-law. It was at the time of *megengan*, a calendrical ceremony, and she had just sent a tray of feast food (*tondjokan*) to her "aunt," who lived next door. Because this was her husband's aunt and her husband's parents were both dead, she considered the aunt a mother-in-law. Juminah said that one should always send a tray of feast food to one's husband's mother, but that the mother-in-law never sends one back. Instead, the daughter-in-law must always go and help cook when the parents-in-law are having a ritual meal, and then the mother-in-law will tell her to help herself to some nice food to take home. If they live far apart, the daughter-in-law comes to help only at the big occasions, the weddings and circumcisions. The same duties apply to the son-in-law. She said that her husband had spent several days at her mother's house a couple of months ago, when her brother got married, building decorations, helping with the butchering, getting chairs, and so on, and had given the boy a number of wedding presents. I asked Juminah what other duties a person has to his parents-in-law, and she said that one ought to visit them once in a while and leave money or clothes. Every time a daughter-in-law cooks or harvests some particularly good food, she should send her parents-in-law some. If she notices that they need new clothes, she should buy some for them. If they are sick, she should buy some medicine that she thinks will make them better. She went on to say that she never liked her own parents-in-law, that they weren't fair. They had always asked her for things, but when her husband went to them for something they always said they had nothing. On the other hand, she thought her own parents were very nice. Whenever she asked for something they would give it if they had it, and her husband was always polite to them and often gave them things.

Such dislike of the parents-in-law is typical, and it is also typical that the conflict is phrased in terms of giving and receiving. If the parents have more money than the children, the balance of the giving is on their side (although the flow of small symbolic presents from the children does not cease); if the children are more fortunate than the parents they are expected to give more than they receive. The parents are ashamed to ask directly for anything, but angry if they do not get what they have in mind. One tradesman told me that he had delayed marrying until after he was thirty-five because his older sister was still not married and he had to support both his sister and his mother. He said that if one marries in such a situation one will find himself in the middle of a conflict between mother and sister and wife. Nowadays, he thought, people with dependent relatives marry more readily than they used to, and these marriages often end in divorce when the wife becomes angry because her husband is giving too much money to his mother.

The strain between parents-in-law and their sons- and daughters-in-law is cushioned by the customs of respect between younger generation and older. These customs encourage and maintain a social distance which both conceals and eases the tensions inherent in the relationship. But respect is not so strongly patterned between affinals of the same generation—brothers- and sisters-in-law; and it was about these relatives that I heard most expressions of hostility, for the Javanese, who rarely express their feelings, find this relationship the least complicated by ambivalent feelings. With these relatives, small disagreements that would be ignored between real relatives seem to set off protracted quarrels in which both parties cease to speak to each other for years on end. For instance, a quarrel between the wives of two neighboring brothers began when one wife asked the ten-year-old servant of the other to come work for her saying that her sister-in-law could not really afford her (which was true, at that time, and that was the reason the insult hurt so much); and from then on for more than ten years the two women never spoke to each other nor sent each other the usual shares of *slametan* feast food, leaving the two brothers and their children to attempt to deal with the breach between the two households as best they could. Another example is the following. During the Indonesian revolution, when the Dutch army occupied Modjokuto, many townsmen fled to their village relatives. My informant, Juminah, with her husband and baby, went to live with her sister, who was married to a peasant. They kept separate budgets and cooked separately, but the sister's husband complained that Juminah was using his wood for her fire. Juminah, taking offense at this criticism, packed up her belongings and went back into town—in spite of her fear of the Dutch soldiers.

The most difficult affinal relationships are those with close relatives—the spouse's nuclear family, and the husbands and wives of one's own primary relatives. Affinal relatives who are more distantly connected are like acquaintances of a slightly higher status; they must be treated with an extra shade of respect. Moreover, such contacts are often useful; business transactions can be arranged through them, or they may serve as intermediaries in marriage arrangements.

Such a polite relationship is typical between the two older couples who are the respective parents of the husband and wife. These two couples are called the *bésan* of each other. A man (or a woman) is the *bésan* of the mother and father of his son- or daughter-in-law, and they are his *bésan*. This term is used only in reference, not in address. It does not imply an alliance between two kin groups, but between the two sets of parents only. There are no obligations or ritual expressions of the relationship, although it is customary to invite *bésan* to all important festivities and to treat them gingerly, with marked over-politeness.

3. HOUSEHOLD COMPOSITION

Variations in Household Make-Up

Marriage in Java is usually monogamous. Polygyny is permitted and carries prestige, but it is rare; when it occurs the households of the wives are usually separate and each is similar in pattern to a monogamous household. It is rare that two mar-

ried couples share the same house. Newly wed couples often live
with the bride's parents until the marriage appears relatively
permanent or until they have the resources to move into a house
of their own, at which time they still usually remain in the neighborhood of at least one set of parents, but there is no formulated
rule of residence after marriage; the choice depends entirely on
personal inclination and opportunity.

Several surveys[3] of household composition revealed the following patterns presented in Table III. It is evident from these
surveys that the nuclear family is indeed the modal household
unit with 58% of the town sample and 75% of the village. A
comparison with a similar analysis of household composition
made in the United States[4] shows that the town Javanese nuclear
family have almost the same degree of "isolation" in household
patterns as Americans: out of a sample of American households
including a married couple, 64% had no adult relatives eighteen
years old and over living in the house; the comparable percentage
for the town Javanese sample is 61%.

The Modjokuto tabulation, however, does not show how
much flux there is in such arrangements. Once a young couple
are established as a separate living unit, their household becomes
the center of a continual process of change. The rhythm of this
process may be slow—as children are born, mature, marry and
leave, or bring a mate to join a household. There may be a series
of brief changes as children not born of the couple come, stay
a year or so, and return to their own parents, or as various single

---

3. The survey of town household composition was made in the following
way: With the guide of a door-to-door census drawn up by the local government (which in spite of its many inaccuracies was a useful starting point for
my investigations), I interviewed nine informants on the composition of each
household in their neighborhood with which they were familiar. The informants had been chosen for their reliability in other matters and for their
gregariousness. This is not a random sample of the town population; the
neighborhoods selected are representative of differing economic levels and
locations. I am fairly certain that the average number of children per house
is underestimated.

The survey of village household composition was made by Robert Jay,
primarily in a village in the Modjokuto Subdistrict, and secondarily in three
other villages outside the area. He followed methods similar to mine.

4. P. C. Glick, "The Family Cycle," *American Sociological Review*, Vol.
XII, No. 2, 1947.

Table III

Variations in Household Composition:
Town and Village Compared

HOUSEHOLD COMPOSITION TYPE	TOWN		VILLAGE	
	Number	*Per Cent*	*Number*	*Per Cent*
1. Simple Nuclear Families:				
a. Husband and wife alone	74			
b. Husband and wife and own children (inc. single adult children)	111		92	
c. Husband and wife and own plus other children (inc. single adult children)	63			
d. One adult and own children (inc. single adult children)	22		22	
Total	270	57.8	114	75
2. Husband and wife and parent	40	8.6	20	12.1
3. Husband and wife and other adult relatives:				
a. Primary	41			
b. Secondary	14			
Total	55	11.8	3	1.9
4. Several Nuclear Families:				
a. Husband and wife and adult child with own child	12			
b. Husband and wife and married child and spouse	14		8	
c. Other sets of married couples	15		1	
Total	41	8.8	9	5.9
5. One adult alone				
a. In own house	17			
b. Renting house space with strangers	29			
Total	46	9.8	7	4.6
6. Groups of consanguineal relatives (no married couple)	15	3.2	—	—
TOTAL HOUSEHOLDS	467		153	
AVERAGE NUMBER OF PEOPLE PER HOUSE:		5.27		
a. ADULTS		3.00		
b. CHILDREN		2.27		

adults attach themselves for a year, ten years, or more. Such processes of change are, of course, present in any kinship system, but they are unusually rapid in Java, chiefly because of the high divorce rate. Although many Javanese divorces are among young people, the couple often have children before separating; and the children are placed, temporarily or permanently, with their grandparents or parent's siblings, or, one parent remarrying, are integrated into a new family with stepparent and half-siblings. In the discussion of the individual in the nuclear family in Chapter Three, it should be understood that although, for the sake of simplicity, relationships only within the nuclear family are described, the Javanese child's world often also includes at various times one or two people, adults or children, who are not his primary relatives.

Usually "a household" is the same as "a group of people who live in a house," but sometimes—particularly in town where living conditions are crowded—there are two households, sometimes related, sharing the same living space but with separate budgets and a sense of separateness. Two sisters and their husbands and children may live together but cook separately, side by side, in the kitchen. Or a young bachelor earning wages in a cigarette factory may lodge with his kin but eat in one of the nearby food stands. In some of the more crowded parts of the town inhabited by a sort of urban proletariat—laborers in the small factories making such things as cigarettes or carbonated drinks or a kind of Javanese potato chip—several unrelated families may live in the same house but maintain completely separate households. It is in such neighborhoods, too, that single adults rent rooms among non-kin or have tiny shacks of their own. Another kind of (paying) addition is groups of students—boys and girls in their late teens—who come from distant villages to attend high school in town.

Adult Relatives in the Household

Adults who join a household, either temporarily or for a long period of time, are usually primary relatives of the husband or wife. Seldom do two economically active married couples live together under one roof; much more common is the addition of an adult who is at the moment unmarried, with or without children. These adults usually make some contribution to the work of the household, either by productive work—a job of some sort —or by helping in the household.

Such dependent or semi-dependent adults are in an embarrassing position. Several very old people who lived with their grown children told me that they never asked their child for anything, simply accepted what was given them, and never interfered in their child's economic arrangements, never gave advice or even know much about the family budget. A grandparent-parent-child triangle often develops, the grandparent doting on the grandchild, giving him things if he can, and questioning the parents' discipline of the child. One man said that once he did not speak to his own mother for three months after she had scolded him for punishing his son for disobedience.

One of the most frequent additions to a household is a grown daughter who is divorced and has not yet remarried. Divorced men usually remarry quite quickly, because they do not feel welcome at home and yet need a woman to perform the indispensable household tasks. A woman, on the other hand, can either maintain herself independently or slip back easily into her parental family, returning to the role of daughter. If a divorcée has a child, the child tends to move into a position almost co-ordinate with hers as a younger sibling, and the grandparents take over at least some aspects of the nurturant role. This was the case, for instance, with Tuti, a woman of about twenty-five who was still married but living at her parental home. Her husband was in the army (a well-respected and popular job among urban lower class) and had been away from home since the first six months of their marriage. Tuti's son Ta, aged one and a half, was the pet of his grandmother, who still had children of her own aged about ten and older. Ta called his grandmother "mother" and his grandfather "father," partly following the usage of his own mother toward them and partly because he was taught so by the affectionate grandmother. His own mother he called by her name, a familiar practice usually only permissible toward kin younger than oneself. Ta seemed to prefer his grandmother to his mother: when his mother went out of the house he did not remonstrate, but when his grandmother left he would weep loudly; all the family would have to perform various stratagems to fool him whenever the grandmother went out. Apparently, the grandmother, because of her dominance over her daughter, was able to shut her out of the child's affections.

A group of close consanguineal kin living in a household together usually acts as a unit, turning over earnings to the head of the household and maintaining the old patterns of parent-child relationships. If, however, there is an affinal relative present —for instance, if the divorced woman and her child should move in with her sister and sister's husband—the group is likely to be less unified. Even though the alliance of the two households is permanent, the divorced woman (who can earn money in some way, often by selling in the market) keeps her finances separate from those of her sister and brother-in-law.

Except for aged parents, who have the accepted right to be taken care of by their child, relatives do not usually stay in a household for any long periods. Or, put another way, since, as one informant put it, women are the "queens of the household," only those relatives who are compatible with the wife are likely to stay long; and it is the wife's relatives who most frequently join the household. In the same survey of households described above, such a preference for kinsmen of the wife was apparent:

Table IV

Adult Relatives in the Household: by Linking Relative

HOUSEHOLD COMPOSITION TYPE	LINKING RELATIVE	
	Wife	Husband
Conjugal couple PLUS:		
wife's primary relatives	45	
husband's primary relatives		31
Conjugal couple PLUS:		
wife's secondary relatives	9	
husband's secondary relatives		5
Conjugal couple PLUS:		
married daughter and son-in-law	11	
married son and daughter-in-law		8
TOTAL HOUSEHOLDS*	65	44

*These figures are not precisely comparable to those in the preceding table, for full information was lacking in a number of cases.

The single adult joining a household usually prefers to live with woman relatives, but in many cases, of course, the economic situation, or simply the fact that there is only one household to join, or personal preference (for instance, for a youngest son—

who is frequently the parents' favorite child) makes the choice of a male relative preferable. One informant had a married son and a married daughter living separately in about equal circumstances, both of whom were willing to take him in. He chose the daughter, he said, because he would feel embarrassed to ask his daughter-in-law to do something for him—such as cook a favorite dish—but felt no embarrassment toward his own daughter. Another informant said that she did not like to have any of her husband's relatives around the house, especially women relatives, because women are always chattering and worrying about the house and two unrelated women will get on each other's nerves. She observed that, since men pay no attention to household matters, it is easier to have a husband's male relatives come to stay; but, she added, most harmonious of all is a household joined only by the wife's kin.

"Borrowed" Children of Kinsmen

Although the touchy nature of affinal connections may be a factor serving to discourage kindred unity, there are a number of important unifying tendencies, one of which is evident in the number of children who are transferred from one family to another. The child who joins a household by such a transfer is most often a nephew or niece of one of the married pair, sometimes a younger sibling or a grandchild.

Javanese see many reasons for bringing the child into the family. Since children are wanted even if only to help in household tasks, a childless couple may ask a brother or sister for one of their children to bring up. One is naturally obliged to provide a home for the child who has lost a parent by divorce or death or whose family is in a comparatively poor financial condition. In the case of a sickly child, a curer may prescribe a change of parents in order to evade the evil spirits that are plaguing him. Then there is the child's education to be considered. The family that lives in a town where the schools are better takes children of relatives during the school year. Village people send their children into towns like Modjokuto to go to elementary school or junior high school. Town people send their children to city relatives to go to better junior high schools and to senior high school.

One informant, Tini, gave me an interesting example. When she was aged four, her older sister got married. Because the government employee whom she married was placed some distance away from her home, and perhaps because she was doubtful about her marriage, the sister asked the mother for Tini, "for company," and brought her up until she finished elementary school. Tini remembers wondering unhappily why her mother didn't want her. After elementary school Tini went to a series of higher schools in several cities, staying with uncles and aunts, while her own parents contributed money for her support. Upon final graduation she returned home to Modjokuto to work in an office and to live with her own mother for the first extended period since she was four years old.

One Modjokuto woman with many children gave one of her sons to her younger sister who lived next door and told her *"Masa bodoa anakku"*—"You can do what you want with my child," meaning that she totally surrendered the child. The boy, Paiman, grew up to feel that the aunt was his mother, and called his aunt "mother" (*mbok*) and his mother "older sister" (*ju*), following the usage of his aunt to her sister. When Paiman was asked teasingly which of the two women would hold his circumcision, he answered assuredly, "Of course '*mbok*' will do it; why should '*ju*' care?" This was a case of complete transfer of affections, accompanied by almost total acceptance of the transfer.

In another instance, a teacher had ten children, and his wife's older brother, who was a fairly high government official in a city nearby and who had no children after twenty years of marriage, asked for a child. A girl was given him when she was three months old. The other children were not told of this transfer, since the girl was now much better off than they and the parents thought they would be jealous. (Actually, in spite of the parents' precautions, the children knew.) The girl was not told of her paternity, and called her parents "aunt" and "uncle."

Adoption of a child is said to bring good luck. Slamet, a young clerk, told me that, because he was sickly, he was given away when he was less than a year old. There were two families

that asked for him, one his mother's older brother and the other
a former wife of the brother who had remarried and lived next
door to his mother. Because of the proximity, Slamet was given
to the former wife even though she was not an actual relative.
The older brother then quarreled and would not speak to Slamet's
mother for a year because of this slight. After Slamet was taken
in he became healthier, and the previously childless couple who
had taken him produced two children. A fourth child was given
them by a pauper neighbor. The couple prospered for a time
and became rich as the operators of the first Javanese-owned
store in Modjokuto. However, he said, the luck brought them
by the two adoptions ran out; they quarreled and were divorced.
After their divorce the fortunes of both declined. Meanwhile,
Slamet's father had died and he went back to live with his real
mother to care for her in her old age. To the Javanese, this family
history would illustrate their belief that adoptions, like marriages, may bring either good luck or bad, depending on whether
the two persons magically suit each other or not.

The distinction between "borrowing" and "adoption" of a
kinsman's child is rather artificial, and not distinctly verbalized
by the Javanese. "Adoption" (*pupon; anak pupon* "adopted
child") is quite clearly defined as the more or less formal re-
linquishment of all claims on the child by the real parents either
by legal statement before witnesses or by their death. What I
have called "borrowing" has no precise Javanese translation.

"Adoption" involves a transfer of rights and obligations—
although these rights and obligations, like most jural matters in
Java, are not rigidly phrased or carefully followed. There is one
primary concern of the parent and the adopting person, kinsman or otherwise: When the child is adult, whom will he support in their old age? The duty of the child to support his parent
in old age is the aspect of the parent-child relationship which is
most emphasized both in discussions of general relationships and
in critical gossip. There are no formal sanctions for enforcing the
obligation, only informal ones, basic to which is recognition by
all concerned that the adoptive parent is indeed the true parent.
Among kinsmen there can simply be mutual agreement as a result of which all participate in perpetuating the desired fiction.

Adoption arrangements between non-kin must be more formal. They may include a payment which is not so much to compensate the real parents for the loss of the child as to protect the adopting parents—that is, to assure that the real parents will not appear when the child is adult and demand him back so that they can profit by his earnings. Such a transaction (*pupon tumbas*, "bought adoption," which in the one case I heard of involved 350 rupiah) must be carried out in the presence of the village headman so that there is a competent witness. One case was reported to me in which the adopting parents gave the real parents some clothes in partial payment, but there was an agreement that in the future the real parents would be given an amount equal to whatever the child gave to the adopting parents. However, when the adopting parents had received the child, they moved away from Modjokuto, left no forwarding address, and were able to bring the child up in complete ignorance of his paternity and therefore get all the benefits of his earnings for themselves.

Inheritance is not seen as a problem in matters of adoption. A child is always eligible to inherit from his real parents but has no intrinsic right to inherit from those who brought him up. However, a child raised solely by an uncle, for instance, may have property settled on him before the death of the uncle in order to avoid conflict with the direct descendants. It is possible, though rare, for the adopted or borrowed child to inherit from both parent and parent surrogate. The handling of inheritance claims is a process of balancing the various demands of the different relatives, a process based not on strict interpretation of a law but on a consideration of situational factors, such as need. A child already provided for by a parent will probably not receive much from his guardian, and vice versa.

Actual adoption (*pupon*) is rare, and adoption by buying is even rarer. When parents die, relatives prefer to keep the children rather than give them to strangers. Sale of children occurs only among exceedingly poor people who can see no other way to raise the child.

More frequent is the practice, which I have called "borrowing," an arrangement by which a child is not considered adopted but is temporarily or permanently cared for by a kinsman of the parent. "Borrowing" of kinsmen's children seems to be based on the unstated assumption that the tie between siblings is such that the children of kinsmen are almost the same as one's own and that therefore affection and care should be given almost as freely to one's nephew as to one's son. Therefore, whenever a sibling needs a child or a child is in need of care which its own parents cannot provide, a loan is made. The parental surrogate may take over complete or partial care of the child, and the relationship may turn out to be permanent, but it is still not *pupon*.

Even though children are freely "lent" among siblings, the Javanese arrangement should not be confused with those of other societies (for instance, the Hopi or Samoans) where the living unit is the extended family and the affections of the child are fractionated among a host of "mothers" and "fathers." The Javanese child discriminates between his uncles and aunts and his real parents. Those older than the parent must be treated with careful respect and distance. When they are younger than the parent and close in age to the child, there is often a warm playful relationship similar to that to the older sibling. The nature of the ties depends on innumerable other factors, such as the age of the child when borrowed, amount of contact with real mother, and personality characteristics.

It is felt that it is much better to give a child to a female relative than to a male relative. It is the woman who will care for the child since the man is away from the house a great deal; and if the child is not a blood-relative of the woman caring for him, she is likely to slight him in favor of her other children. A story was related to me which illustrates this. There was a childless couple in Modjokuto who took into their house two boys, one the nephew of the husband and one the nephew of the wife. When the husband's nephew asked to be circumcised, he was given a small ceremony and, as is customary, a new *sarung* (men's skirt-like garment). Sometime later the husband had no clothes to wear, and the wife gave him the boy's *sarung*, indicating a disregard for the boy's rights. The next year when the wife's nephew asked to be circumcised, she insisted on giving him a very big ceremony, going deeply into debt, and gave him two new *sarungs*, thus demonstrating her greater concern for her own kin.

The most satisfactory arrangement, apparently, is the "borrowing" of the child by the mother's sister, and this is by far the most popular of these arrangements. The next most frequent temporary foster parent is the child's own older sister, and following her the child's maternal grandparents.

The relationship between child and parental surrogate varies widely. If the real parents are still living the child usually maintains some ties, as in the case of Slamet, who, after having been fed, clothed, and schooled by neighbors, returned to his mother in her old age to care for her. On the other hand, there are children who reject their own mother and, when told that she is the real mother, refuse to believe it.

Stepchildren

The combination of a high divorce rate and a high death rate results in a large proportion of Javanese children living with only one parent, usually the mother. Since a single woman who chooses to keep her dependent child or children with her will usually have to move in with another family in order to provide a good home in which to bring up a child, she usually moves in with some of her relatives—her mother or sister or aunt. She may remarry, in which case she may have more children, half-siblings to those from the first marriage.

The Javanese find the latter situation a very difficult one for all concerned; although usually "successful" by dint of the conscious efforts of everyone, there is always strain. Women who have stepchildren are very conscious of the fact that they must show no sign of favoritism to their own children for fear that the stepchildren or the husband will be resentful. In this connection, one informant, a widower with five young children, described the difficulties he was having with his present wife, a well-meaning amiable woman. He began by saying that children never consider their stepmother in the same way they consider their own mother. They are more disobedient to the stepmother than they would be to their own mother. When his wife told her stepchildren to go somewhere for her, they just answered "It's too hot, I don't feel like going," and then she felt slighted. He felt that they should have more respect for her, as they would have had for their own mother. He then went on in detail. His wife did not like the children to have better clothes than she (in contrast to a real mother, who would want the children to have the best) because she felt that would represent their superiority to her. His wife had a niece, her sister's child, whom she had brought up as her own; and she always bought nice clothes for herself and her niece but not for her stepchildren. One of these, a girl of about sixteen, felt very hurt when the stepmother bought her niece some earrings. Typically, she did not tell her father, for that would upset him, but instead stayed in her room and wept till one of her younger brothers saw her and told her father about it. He in turn said nothing directly to his wife about it, but gave her long lectures on Javanese mystical philosophy (in which he was an expert), using the family relationships as examples for the moral rules he expounded, and finally hinted that she should buy her stepdaughter a pair of earrings. The family picture he presented was one of a complex network of interpersonal tensions (expressed mainly in attitudes toward material matters—clothing and jewelry) accompanied by great concern for restraint in order to protect the father from being upset (which he was anyway) and skillful use of various indirect means of communication (weeping, philosophy).

Both the stepchildren and the mother are blamed for conflicts within the Javanese family, but a stepfather is rarely blamed. There are a number of folk tales centering on the evil stepmother theme, the most well known being the story of "Brambang Abang and Bawang Putih," which are the names of two little girls (humorous names, meaning "Red Onion" and "White Garlic"). Every child knows this story, of which one version goes as follows:

There was once a man and his wife. Each had been married before, and each had a child from the previous marriage. Bawang Putih was the daughter of the husband and Brambang Abang was the daughter of the wife. The husband was often away from home, and when the wife fed the children she gave her own child good food and her stepchild weeds to eat. When she fed them rice, she gave a great deal to her own child but only a little to the stepchild. When the child protested, the stepmother rubbed rice all over the child's face, so that when she went to her father to complain that she was not being fed enough rice the stepmother was able to say, "Look, she's had so much that she's smeared it all over her face." And so the father did not believe Bawang Putih.

Eventually the wife had a baby, and Bawang Putih had to help her stepmother while Brambang Abang just played in the yard. One day when Bawang Putih was washing the baby's clothes in the river, a piece of clothing was carried away by the current. The stepmother was angry and sent the child off, telling her not to come back until she had found the garment. Bawang Putih wandered a long while, following the river, until she encountered the Green Giant of the River. This was a very fearful encounter, but finally the Green Giant gave her the piece of clothing and she returned home with it.

When Bawang Putih grew up, she became a very good person, whereas Brambang Abang grew up stupid, unable to do anything useful, because all she had done all her life was play.

Here is a tale which I was told was a record of events which supposedly took place in a town about fifty miles from Modjo-kuto:

There was a married couple, each of whom had been married before and had a child from the previous marriage—the man a son, and the woman a daughter. The wife was unfaithful to her husband, and her stepson, finding it out threatened to tell his father about her lover. The stepmother killed the child, cut him up into pieces, cooked him, and served him up to his father. When the man asked his wife what kind of meat it was, the wife replied, "Never mind, just eat it." He asked again and she answered in the same way. So he ate it. When he had finished the meal, his little stepdaughter came in and innocently made a remark which caused the father to suspect what the truth was. He went into the kitchen and looked in the pot, and there was the head of his son.

Such extreme fantasies, centered on the bad stepmother, are a reflection of the prevalent Javanese view that conflicts within the household focus on the woman since her role is the hardest to perform and she is likely to make the most mistakes. Juminah, an informant, told me about a family in which there was a man and wife and two daughters of the man. While the girls were still young the house was fairly calm; but as they grew up and dared to oppose their stepmother and complain to their father, the atmosphere became very stormy, and the stepmother repeatedly left her husband and returned for a time to her own family. Juminah said that whenever there is a quarrel in that kind of family, the stepmother chooses the father over the children, whereas if she were the real mother of the children she would always side with her children. If the wife and the stepchildren quarrel, they end with not speaking to each other, but a real mother would never cease to speak to her own children. She would always make up with them soon after a quarrel. It is much easier, she said, if the children are those of the wife and the husband is their stepfather, because a woman is with the children all the time, while the father is in the house only occasionally. If her own children are naughty, the mother can keep the father from knowing and can tell him only their good side; but if she has stepchildren, she not only does not hide the children's bad side but also complains to the father about them, and there is always fighting in the house.

The Central Role of Women in Household Composition

It is clear from the foregoing discussion that there is considerable variation in the composition of Javanese households. The modal household consists of a single elementary family, but the make-up of the remaining households is quite varied. The survey of village households showed a simpler distribution than the town, with nuclear family households making up 75% of the total, and an additional 12% consisting of nuclear family households with the addition only of a parent of one of the spouses. The town survey, on the other hand, revealed a much lower percentage of nuclear family households, with the remainder more evenly distributed. The difference here between town and village is probably due first to the fact of a housing shortage in the town which forces people to double up together who normally might not. Secondly, it may be that able-bodied villagers who are unmarried or widowed move into town in search of employment and stay with town relatives. And thirdly, some of the differences between the two surveys must be due to sampling variations.

When the composition of those households in the town which do not conform to the mode are examined, and the qualitative material concerning attitudes toward various members of the kindred and toward various affinal relatives is studied, there seems to be a distinct emphasis on maternal connections. That is to say, in cases where two nuclear families join within a single household, or where single adults are attached to a nuclear family household, the linking relative is more often a woman than a man. When children are adopted, permanently or temporarily, those related to the wife rather than to the husband are generally preferred. These of course are statements of numerical frequency, and can be corroborated only by means of a household census which is based on proper sampling procedures and statistical methods which take such demographic factors into account as the longer life expectancy of women. However, the numerical data we have bolster our conclusion that the woman in the Javanese family is the crucial link to other kinsmen. More compelling than the quantitative evidence is the material on Javanese attitudes in these matters.

We have already mentioned the prevalent Javanese opinion that, for the sake of household harmony, if one is forced to take relatives into one's home, it is much better to take those who are kinsmen—or, even better, kinswomen—of the wife, rather than of the husband. There is also the marked preference women have for adopting, or caring for, children of their own relatives, rather than those of their husband's relatives. Further, there is the strong feeling that after divorce, the children should remain with the mother, even though she may remarry several times, with the result grown children have considerably stronger ties to their mothers than to their fathers. And, there is a tendency for daughters, after their marriage, to maintain a closer relationship with their parents and to return to live with them if divorced, while sons tend to drift away emotionally, and rarely return home as adults.

For, to anticipate for the moment, there is a general, informal, largely unverbalized avoidance between the adult men of a Javanese family—between father and son, and between brothers. In addition, the husband and father often appears to withdraw his attention from household affairs, and to keep emotionally as uninvolved as he can. The woman or women of the household have a free field within which to operate in the domestic domain. The wife makes most of the decisions; she controls all family finances, and although she gives her husband formal deference and consults with him on major matters, it is usually she who is dominant. Strong-willed men may have a relationship of equal partnership with their wives, but families actually dominated by the man are exceedingly rare.

The position of women in Javanese society generally is very strong. Most occupations—including many types of minor farm labor, petty trade, wholesale buying and selling, small manufacturing, domestic service and teaching—are open to them. Women can own farm land and supervise its cultivation. Thus a woman has no difficulty supporting herself and her children, should she want to. Men, on the other hand, don't do household work such as cooking, and rarely live alone, or bring up their children themselves. Because of the rather uneasy relationship between fathers and sons, and between brothers, a divorced or widowed man is loath to return to his parental home, and usually seeks another wife quite quickly. A divorced or widowed woman, however, can live alone if she wants, or because of her firm ties to her parents and sisters, can join their households with little strain.

All these diverse factors, working simultaneously—the dominant status of the woman in the family, the attitudes of restraint and avoidance between the men of the family, the contrasting closeness of the women of the family, the mistrust of affinal relatives generally, and the strong economic position of women—all work together to produce a matrifocal pattern of familial relationships which is most clearly evident in household composition, one of a solidary core of related women with a loose periphery of the men of the family.

4. PROPERTY DIVISION AT DIVORCE AND AT DEATH

The Settlement Process

The Javanese method for settling conflicting claims to property in the event of divorce or death is not based on an appeal to an impersonal legal prescription which can be interpreted and applied to any individual case with an assurance that the final outcome will be just. It is based, rather, on a direct consideration of the particular merits and strengths of each claim, together with other situational aspects of the particular case, the aim being not to achieve an abstract justice necessarily but to reach a solution on which all participants agree. Unanimity of opinion is sought rather than "correct" answers. For instance, there is a rule, with which any Javanese is familiar, that on the death of a parent the sons inherit twice as much as the daughters; this is the Islamic law, the informant will explain, while the "real Javanese" law is that all children, male and female, inherit equally. But when one investigates some particular case, one may find that both rules have been ignored and that the youngest of the children, who still are not able to earn their own living, or the girls, who may need to have economic freedom to divorce their husbands, have been given the entire inheritance, while their older siblings take nothing.

The common method, then, of reaching the solution of settlement cases is an extended talking out of all claims, sometimes with mediators, until—each side giving way a little—agreement is reached. There may be a concealed residue of hard feelings on the part of those who feel that they have been forced to give too much ground, but this residue is far less in cases which have been handled in the traditional manner than in those in which the matter has been taken to court. For the possibility of going to the government court at the regency capital is always present; and there are "lawyers" *(pokrol* or *adpokat)*, usually Chinese, who can—with or without legal proceedings—push for a more rationalistic solution, in which one side wins completely and the other loses. Most Javanese feel, and possibly rightly, that the court expenses will outweigh the possible gain and that the presence of a "lawyer" means more interpersonal friction than is desired. Many villages refuse to allow such a lawyer to live among them for this reason.

The traditional way of resolving conflicts between individuals is effective because of the strength of the Javanese value represented by the word *rukun*. *Rukun* is an ideal standard for social relationships, meaning harmony, co-operation, unity of effort, minimization of conflicts. It is the state striven for at all times in a family, neighborhood, village, in any enduring group. This valued state is often described by Javanese, particularly city people, in idealized platitudes, suggesting an almost mystical submersion of the individual in the group, which make it seem an unrealistic empty word. But *rukun*, to the peasant who lives by it, means a hard-headed *modus vivendi* reached through a process of give-and-take between self-interested people.

The direct expression of self-interest is constrained by a desire for *rukun*. This value not only guides the participants in their discussions toward compromise but also restrains them from expressions of antagonism and hostility, inducing them to try to maintain an appearance of harmony throughout the process of negotiation. A concern for *rukun* makes it necessary for the opposing parties to relinquish those personal desires likely to cause overt social disturbance.

Within the kin group, the exercise of self-interest is even further constrained by a complex of moral values and affections coloring the relationships, and—especially among primary kin—concern for self tends to become merged with concern for others. Among siblings or between children and their surviving parent, inheritance conflicts are rare; they usually arise only when no primary relatives remain, such as between the surviving childless wife of a dead man and his siblings, or between the deceased's brother and grandson, the son having died previously.

The process of settling claims is thus animated and given form by the value of *rukun* as both means and end. It is implemented in practice by the public nature of these matters: all transfers of property, to be permanent, must be reported to the village head, and his approval is required for any legal record of the transfer. A village head can, if backed by public opinion, obstruct a decision that he feels is unfair, especially to any weak claimants, such as young children; he can advise in cases of apparent deadlock, and he can mediate between hostile parties. In his decisions, the official refers to two bodies of customs concerning property transfer: the Arabic-Islamic customs, which give greater weight to the agnatic line over all other relatives, and the traditional Javanese customs *(adat)*, which give equal weight to both male and female relatives, bilaterally reckoned. Usually the latter set of customs is more important in the minds of those who are making a decision. Even devout *santris* who consider it their duty to follow Islamic law will follow it only in part. For instance, they may distribute rice fields according to the Islamic measure of two to the sons and one to the daughters, but the house-land equally among all children. The contrast between the two types of law can easily be overemphasized. For most Javanese they are not alternative ideologies (except where the Moslem–anti-Moslem split is so intensified that this difference is but one more symbol of social division) but, rather, alternative interpretations, both of which are less important than the characteristics of the particular problem at hand.

Customary solutions have a force of their own: the very fact that many people have, in the past, followed a certain path makes it easier for later arrivals to perceive the path as suitable to their values and desires. For this reason it is common, for instance, to divide the estate equally among all children of the deceased, and deviations from this rule are seen as resulting from special considerations.

Settlement at Divorce

Since divorce is a break and realignment of social relationships that is rarely amicable, an amiable settlement is difficult. Because of this, property division upon divorce is handled in a more legalistic way than inheritance.

The most important legal concept for understanding both divorce settlement and inheritance in Java is that of the distinction between the community property of husband and wife, on the one side, and their separately owned personal property on the other. Since husband and wife are an economic unity, even though the wife may not participate directly in the acquisition of income, her performance of household tasks is considered part of the productive economic enterprise. For this reason all goods acquired during the marriage, other than by inheritance, are thought to be "community property" *(gana-gini)*. This is the property that is divided up at divorce.

The separately owned "personal property" of each spouse is that which he had at the time of marriage or any property which he inherits during the marriage. This personal property never passes to the marriage partner at divorce or death. (If, however, during the marriage the personal property—a rice field owned by the wife, for instance—is jointly worked by husband and wife, the year-by-year produce from that property is considered "community property.") Personal property of this sort has no special Javanese term: it is sometimes called "brought-in things," *barang bektan*, or "own property," *duwèké déwé*.

At divorce, personal property is retained and community property is divided in the ratio of two parts to the husband and one part to the wife. This is usually expressed as proportionate to the amount a man can carry, since the masculine method of carrying heavy burdens is in two baskets at each end of a shoulder-pole, while the woman's way of carrying burdens is in one basket on her back. The Javanese expression for the divorce settlement formula is *sapikul, sagéndong:* one shoulder-pole to one basket on the back. If, however, one of the parties to the divorce is clearly in the wrong, the entire community property may be granted to the wronged person; and I know both of cases in which the man kept all the property and sent his unfaithfull wife off with nothing, and cases in which the woman kept the property, giving the husband nothing.

The basic principles underlying this distinction between personal and community property are, first, that, since husband and wife are economically an indivisible unit and both contribute to this whole, neither has any claim to any piece of property gained during the marriage period by virtue of his working alone for it; and, second, that neither gives up his independence and separateness; the woman surrenders no property that was her own or her family's to her husband. Property received from consanguineal kin can be passed on only to consanguineal kin.

Arguments at divorce settlement do not dispute these premises. The bone of contention is usually whether a piece of property is community or personal property. Especially after a long marriage the lines become blurred; for instance, if a piece of inherited land is sold to buy a cow with the addition of money from the common pool, which category does the cow enter? The following is an example of this kind of case and also illustrates the situational character of solutions and the role of the village head. A woman left her husband to marry another man. Most of the property they had, a house and land, was hers, given her by her parents, but she had unthinkingly let her husband register the property in his name. After the divorce the husband, on the grounds of the registration, claimed all the property, and the wife asserted that, in spite of the registration, it was hers. The village head decided not to divide the property at all but to put it in trust for the three children, who were living with neither parent but with a grandparent. This was a solution which protected the children, and was acceptable to all.

Settlement at Death

The same distinction between community owned and personal property enters into inheritance settlements, but only if there are no children. If a person dies without issue, his personal property "returns" to his parents and siblings, and the community property should be divided according to the 2:1 ratio, his consanguineal relatives receiving his share, although often this is not done. If there are children, they have claim to all the property of both parents, which is usually divided equally among them.

A widow has no right to her husband's personal property, and, by Islamic law, has a right to only a small portion of their community property. However, if there are children, they are entitled to receive all their father's property at his death. If they are still young, or even if adult and not in need of the property, the mother will keep it in trust for them, and it may not be officially divided up until her death (especially in the many cases where there is little to divide). When there is a great deal of property, it is usually divided among the children, and the mother is given a portion of land to support her until her death. Often she continues to own the house and her youngest child continues to live there with her, caring for her until her death, when he inherits the house. If the couple are peasants, a portion of their rice land may be not actually owned by them, but "lent" them by the village in return for various community services such as voting and road repair. The right to use this land *(gogol)* may be passed from parent to child, but the land is not considered the same as other inherited land. It usually goes to the widow, and at her death to one of the children.

The transfer of property to descendants is a continual process in Java; it does not occur solely at death. Throughout a man's life he gives his children portions of his property. If he owns land, he gives portions to his children as they mature and have children. All such gifts are taken into account when the remaining property is finally divided up at his death. Often when a man becomes too old to manage his affairs, he distributes all his property and keeps only a fraction to support him during his old age, usually giving that fraction finally to the child who cares for him.

Since inheritance involves less contention than divorce, the rules are likely to be less closely followed. The main concern is that no kin be without a minimal means of support. Unless the deceased had already stated his wishes before he died, the immediate kin usually get together and decide among themselves the disposition of the property. If a man has an adopted child or is bringing up a kinsman's child, he usually gives that child some property before he dies in order to make sure that he is provided for. Parents are often more concerned about their daughters than their sons, feeling that girls are more dependent on their family and that boys can always take care of themselves; and they often tell everyone concerned that they want the girl to get the major part of the property.

If one of a group of siblings takes over an indivisible piece of property, he should then pay the rest in cash for their share of it. However, this payment is usually quite a bit less than the property is worth on the open market, and the rationale given is that the selling brother can always expect to come back to the piece of land if he needs to; in other words, sale of property between close kin is never final. In fact, these arrangements among siblings are rarely legalized, partly because of the expense of registration and partly because of the temporary nature of the transaction. For this reason, when a piece of inherited land is sold to an outsider, it is usually necessary to inform all near kin in order to avoid later disputes.

The village religious official, the *modin*, is usually consulted in inheritance problems, and sometimes the village head, the *lurah*, is also asked for advice. Their decisions carry some weight, but if there continues to be dissension among the heirs the case can be taken to the religious official at the subdistrict level, the *naib*. He can decide nothing, inheritance being considered not a religious but a civil matter (unlike divorce settlement, which is under his authority); but he can give informed advice and can help to bring about a compromise agreement. Many people feel that it is best not to try to go above him because the civil court will probably decide in the same direction the *naib* did, and court costs can be great.

Here are some examples of typical inheritance settlements: One informant, a woman schoolteacher, had a younger brother who was also a schoolteacher and an older brother who was a government official. When their parents died, the three were living separately and away from their original home, where there were two large houses. When the three came to discuss their inheritance, the older brother said that he did not want the property divided. The others agreed, but only one, the younger brother, was living near the family home, and so he moved into the family property. My informant said she didn't care, that perhaps when she was old and no longer working she would like to move back to the family house, but until then it was all right for her brother to keep the house. But she did not like the brother's wife. She said that she had wanted to take some of the movable things out of her parents' house, such as chinaware, but when she went to visit she found that her sister-in-law was already using it. This made her angry, but her husband counseled her to say nothing. As a result she now never visits her younger brother. This is a typical example of the *rukun* ideal in practice, resulting in external harmony at the expense of repression of true feelings.

Another informant told me that her grandfather had divided up all his land equally among his daughters and sons, leaving only a small piece for himself. In his last sickness a granddaughter nursed him, and he wanted to give her that last piece of land. At the funeral, the religious official was told of this wish, and when everything was finished and everyone was gathered in the front yard about to set off for the cemetery, the bier already on the shoulders of the mourners, the official stood up and announced that the piece of land was going to the little girl and then waited for objections. There were none, and the inheritance was taken as agreed. However, no actual registration of the land transfer was made, and some years later the girl was still not in possession of the land, the kinsman whose land adjoined it was harvesting the fruits from it, and there was talk that he wanted to register it in his name.

In another case there were four siblings, three women and a man, all married. The three women had moved away from the village; the man had married a village girl and remained near home. Their mother had said that she wanted her son, who was the youngest and her favorite, to have the house and rice land. Therefore, when the parents died, it was agreed among the four that the son should have the land and pay the others for their shares. This turned out to be a very amicable arrangement, a genuine *rukun*.

5. MARRIAGE

Marriage Arrangement

A wedding is a pivotal moment, a point in time at which kinship relationships are extended and changed. In Java, it marks the formation of a new nuclear family which will soon separate itself, economically and spatially, from the parent group, and form the basis for a new household. In some societies the wedding also represents the lateral extension of ties between two unrelated corporate groups or the reaffirmation of membership in one common endogamous group; but in Java only two nuclear families are concerned, the two that will eventually be united through the possession of a common grandchild. The members of the wider kindred on each side remain in the background, supporting, contributing, helping, witnessing, each according to his particular relationship to the parents of the newly-wed pair.

Thus, in Java, marriage is not thought of as the joining together of two widely spread networks of kinsmen. What is stressed by the Javanese is the establishment of a new, autonomous household. This point of view is evident in the usual term for "getting married," *omah-omahan*, which is derived from *omah*, "house." Also related are the words for "household," *somahan*, which means, approximately, "that which is connected with one house," and for "spouse," in polite speech, *sémah*. In practice, the actual economic and residential independence of a newly-married couple from their parents' households may be delayed for a year or more after marriage, and it is not until this has finally occurred that the couple is socially considered to be married. In a sense, therefore, the actual closing of the marriage contract, in Java, can be seen to comprise a series of steps, which may take some time to complete.

Most marriages are arranged by the parents of the couple. They select the future spouse and decide the date of the wedding, particularly in the case of the first marriage of their child. Javanese believe that this is the proper way for entering marriage, and that the younger people ought to acquiesce unquestioningly to the decisions of their parents. Only the mother and father, however, and no other kinsmen are usually allowed to make this decision for them. There is rarely any preference for choosing the spouse from among relatives, and, with certain exceptions, few prohibitions for marriage among secondary kinsmen.

Thus, parental marriage arrangement in Java must be seen not in terms of kinship organization as such, but as an aspect of the economic and prestige systems of the larger society, and as a function of the internal authority structure of the elementary family. For the choice of spouse, especially at the time of the first marriage, serves the interests of the parents primarily, by expanding the range of their social ties, or consolidating those already existing, and by validating their social rank in their community. Within the family, the fact that the child must surrender the choice of his spouse to his parents is a symbol of his social and psychological dependency on them, of his acceptance of his future responsibilities toward them in their old age, and of his lesser status in regard to them.

The first marriage for a daughter is often arranged soon after her first menstruation. An early marriage is sought for her especially if she begins to show a marked interest in men, for her parents are concerned that she does not build a reputation for loose morals. Such a reputation, suggesting that she would not be a faithful wife, would diminish her chances of landing a good responsible husband, with sufficient social prestige. In traditional families, the problem was solved by marrying daughters off before puberty, even as young as nine or ten. These little girls would move into their husband's home, to be brought up by him and the mother-in-law, and it would be her new family's concern, no longer her parents', to keep her away from other men. Today this practice is rare, and the age of marriage for girls appears to be gradually increasing. Probably most Javanese girls have been married—at least briefly—by the time they are sixteen or seventeen. Very few never marry at all.

Boys usually do not marry until they are more mature and can satisfactorily support a family. This age is variable; it may be anywhere between eighteen and thirty. Bachelors over thirty are extremely rare. Sons have more control over their fate than daughters do: parents usually wait until their son feels himself ready for marriage and comes to them for help. They often allow him to indicate the girl he wants or to veto their suggestions. Once he has done this however, his parents do all the negotiating with the girl's parents, and make the wedding arrangements.

In a great many cases—perhaps most—the first meeting of husband and wife-to-be occurs at the wedding ceremony. A high proportion of first marriages end in divorce. Second and third marriages are arranged with less formality and more participation on the part of the couple themselves. Even when the couple to be married freely choose one another, they usually are only briefly and casually acquainted. Today, with increasing higher education for both boys and girls, and the concomitant delay of marriage, young couples more and more meet in school, and marry on the basis of considerably longer acquaintance.

Selection of Mate

No matter who makes the selection, it is not one which is rigidly prescribed by custom. There are a few minor prohibitions on marriage with certain kinsmen and certain magical considerations which must be observed. Geographical proximity is not so important; even in village populations a wife or husband is often brought in from another village, and among the better-off townspeople the distance between the homes of the two families may be fifty miles or more. Above all, the most important single factor operating to channel selection of a spouse is that of social rank or class. Second to class, and allied to it, is religious orientation, that is, relative emphasis on strongly Moslem, animistic, or Hindu-Buddhist mystic beliefs. All of these considerations are ignored occasionally in practise: prohibited kinsmen do sometimes marry, magically inpropitious weddings are carried out, difference in social rank or in religious persuasion is now and then overridden.

Social class is always a matter of great concern. If there is inequality between the families of husband and wife it will be a constant source of tension. Usually similarity in status is assured by the many automatic mechanisms which govern relationships every day in the continual jockeying for recognition of position. A young man who wants to marry, or his parents, would approach only those families which could cause them the least status-embarrassment. Even in rural areas, where the range of prestige differences is small, this is still of concern, and in some traditional village circles there is a marriage-broker *(ḍanḍan)*, whose main function is to mediate and smooth over any delicate matters of disparity in rank.

In the town, considerations of relative rank are more pressing, perhaps because of the greater class mobility and the greater differentiation of classes and subclasses. A popular play *(ludrug)* performed in Modjokuto by a troupe from Surabaya dramatized the conflict of class and affection: A son of a respectable govern-

ment official falls in love with one of the servants and marries
her without his parents' knowledge. In time the parents, who live
in another city, arrange a highly suitable marriage with the
daughter of an even higher official, and on coming to inform the
boy discover to their horror that he is already married. The
father goes into a rage, calls the son's wife an "animal" (the worst
insult possible to a Javanese), and sends her off with some money.
The son then is in a conflict situation: shall he choose the upper
class wife or follow his affections? In keeping with Javanese
values, he chooses the upper class girl and prospers ever after.

In general young people marry only with the consent of their
parents, and the two cases I heard of in Modjokuto where there
was direct defiance of parental disapproval involved differing
social positions. In both these cases the young people had met in
school: In the first case, a girl who was the only child of parents
with a princely title of the lowest rank *(Radèn)* married a
schoolmate with no title; the parents were opposed because, since
titles descend in the male line only, with this marriage to a com-
moner meant that the title would be lost to the family. In the
second case there was a secret marriage between a girl from the
family of a high official and a poor schoolmate who, though of
lowly family, had prospects of a promising government career
because of his high education.

With the recent shifts in the political structure of Indonesia,
the occupational system is changing rapidly, and it is becoming
more and more possible for people of lower-class origin to move,
by way of education, into white-collar governmental positions,
which, as in the past, are the occupations of highest prestige. The
aspirations of the young people are changing, and most share the
views of the little twelve-year-old girl who, in spite of the fact
that all of her kin were peasants and craftsmen, told her mother,
"I don't want a husband who is just a carpenter like Daddy.
When you look for a man for me, look for someone with a
salary, like a soldier." (A visit to Modjokuto four years later
found this girl married to a schoolteacher.)

Kinship prohibitions on the choice of marriage partner are
few, and there is very little agreement of opinion among Javanese about them. Discussions about incest as such—sexual rela-

tionships among primary relatives—are remarkably low in emotional tone; and, although I could find no verifiable cases of such unions, a number of people told me seriously that children of the same mother by different fathers could marry. Several informants, when asked whether an uncle and niece might marry, said they didn't know; some assured me that it was permissible but added, "I wouldn't allow it in my family." One spoke with considerable repugnance at the thought, saying that it was just as bad as brother-and-sister incest.

There is some feeling, perhaps stronger in the past, that a man who is classificatory "son" to a woman, whatever their relative age, should not marry her, and the same for a man who is "younger brother" to a woman. However, I knew of a number of marriages in Modjokuto which went against this latter tradition. Informants stated that it didn't matter if the man was classificatory "father" to his wife (which would be the case of uncle marrying niece), but I found no cases of this kind of marriage in Modjokuto.

The only rule on which there appeared to be complete unanimity among all informants was that parallel cousins on the father's side should never marry. This, they explain, is due to the law that a girl's father, father's brother, brother, or in the absence of these, father's brother's son, is her guardian *(wali)* and is responsible for giving her away in marriage. The rule is referred to as *pantjer wali,* literally "guardian in direct line." (Curiously, informants called this an Islamic law, which it could hardly be since marriage with the father's brother's son is *preferred* not prohibited among Arabic groups.)

Stepsiblings, that is, children of a married couple by previous marriages, can and do marry, subject to the Islamic restriction that they must not have been suckled at the same breast. Cousin marriages, except between patrilateral parallel cousins, are very frequent, although there is disagreement as to their desirability. Poor urban people with *abangan* outlook (i.e., the animistic variant of Javanese values) often feel that marriages should be kept outside the kindred because, otherwise, if the marriage results in divorce, the already unsteady relationship between kin will be overly strained and the two sides of the family (for instance, two siblings whose children have married and divorced) will not speak to each other for years. On the other hand, upper class people *(prijaji)*, who tend to have a lower divorce rate and who have more property to keep in the family, are often very much in favor of such endogamous marital ties.

It is usually thought that a younger brother or sister should postpone marriage till after the older sibling, especially an older sister, is married, but this restriction is often ignored or evaded. If the family is traditionally oriented, there is a ritual way out: at the time of the wedding, a man is found who goes through a mock marriage with the older sister at the same time that the younger sister gets married. This ritual is called *nglangkahi gunung,* "stepping over the mountain."

An important magical restriction on choice of mate which is observed by even the best educated people in Modjokuto has to do with the dates of birth of the couple. As soon as serious marriage negotiations are under way, both families confer with a man who knows about such things to see if the birth dates of the couple are in harmony, for it is believed that compatibility between their birth dates, as indications of their characters, is essential to compatibility in their marriage. The method for computing this *(pétungan)* is rather complex, but most Javanese have some knowledge of it and consider its results significant. Cases where couples marry in spite of a bad augury are rare. Since ways of computing the divination differ the occasion can be exploited in order to politely evade an undesirable match; the suitor is simply told that the dates are not harmonious, a fact which is supposed to imply no derogatory personal criticism.

In sum, then, the patterns of selection of mate are highly variable. Here are details of some marriages in Modjokuto which illustrate the various points made above. (Note the distances involved, which result in a scatter of kinsmen over a wide geographic area.)

1. A girl from a wealthy village family married a man from a town some two hundred miles away. The marriage came about because the husband of the girl's older sister also came from that town but, after marriage, had moved to Modjokuto, and the man, who was one of his relatives, visited him often for about two years

and finally asked his parents to write to her parents to ask for her hand.

2. A girl from a family of urban laborers was brought up by an older brother. The brother had an adopted son to whom he married the girl.

3. A son of a wealthy Surabaya family asked his grandmother (being the youngest son of her youngest son, he was her favorite grandson) to find him a wife because, he said, if anything went wrong he could blame someone else, not himself. She found him the daughter of a friend in another city.

4. A boy in the army had a close friend from an urban family of small market tradesmen. The friend showed him a photograph of his sister. The boy arranged his marriage to the sister by mail, seeing the girl for the first time at the wedding.

5. A daughter of a cigarette-stand man in the Modjokuto market was first married to an acquaintance of her mother's family in a town fifteen miles away when she was eight years old. There was a big marriage celebration, but when she was taken to her new mother-in-law's house she cried, and two days later she was allowed to go home to her own parents. She was again married off when she was sixteen to a prosperous cloth salesman who toured through Modjokuto once a week from a town some hundred miles away. This marriage was arranged by her parents without telling her. On the day of the wedding she was taken to the man's house in Modjokuto by her girl friends, but she refused to spend the night there and went home with them. She did not like her husband because he was too old for her. He was ashamed and went back to his own town. The third and last time, her father arranged to marry her to an attractive young tailor of her own age who had been a childhood playmate. Her father lectured her on making the marriage last, and it was a successful marriage.

6. A young woman, after three one-day affairs similar to those in the preceding case, was married to her father's older sister's son, an older policeman, who needed her to care for his three children whose mother was dead. She felt happy in this arrangement because, she said, her mother-in-law was her own aunt.

7. Two men who were fellow workers on the railroad arranged for their two children, aged twelve and eight, to marry. The eight-year-old girl moved two hundred yards away from her own home to her mother-in-law's house and was brought up by her, but she often went home to ask for presents from her father. This marriage lasted for more than forty years, with the exception of one year when the man divorced her, married another woman temporarily, and then, dissatisfied, returned to the first wife.

Courtship and Engagement

The Javanese pattern of correct formal courtship involves three steps. First, some kind of preliminary negotiations are made by a friend or relative of the young man in order to avoid the embarrassment of being refused. Second, with at least a polite reception assured, a formal visit is paid to the girl's house by the young man, accompanied by his father or other relatives. This visit is called *nontoni*, "to look at," its purpose being to give the man and girl a chance to see each other and, perhaps more important, to give the parents of both an opportunity to size each other up. Traditionally, and frequently even today, neither of the two young people knows the other, and this is their only chance to make an appraisal.

Formal calling is an art lovingly cultivated by the Javanese. Bearing, gesture, facial expression, modulation of voice, and, especially, selection of vocabulary are all studiedly stylized, and a fine performer is a delight to watch. It is an art practiced for its own sake. The content is a barrier to perfection, an intrusive element that disturbs the exquisitely refined surface pattern of the conversation. Very gradually, piece by piece, by subtle allusion or euphemism, the burden of the message appears—and only after several hours of seemingly idle verbal play.

In most Modjokuto houses the father receives male visitors, inviting them to sit with him at a table in the front room. The women visitors go to one side of the main front room if there is space, or out back with the women of the house. Women's conversation is likely to be less careful and subtle unless they are new acquaintances. The role of the girl, object of all this ceremony, is confined to silent serving of tea or coffee and snacks, and she usually is intensely embarrassed at the presence of her possible husband. The girl is supposed to walk with eyes shyly downcast. A man looking over a girl is said to pay special attention to her eyes and to the way she walks. If she looks around too much, if she does not walk demurely, these are signs that she will be disobedient and willful, and he may decide against her.

It is obvious that, in these circumstances, the traits for which a girl is chosen or rejected are likely to be superficial. One government official told me that he rejected a girl because her feet were too big. At any rate, the important factor, even on the man's side, is usually the wishes of the parents. Very young people cannot easily oppose their parents' desires and rarely do. Sometimes the girl is asked her feelings, but often she is not even told the purpose of the social call; and she may not learn of her approaching wedding until a day or two before it is to take place.

The formal request for the girl's hand may come either before or after the boy sees her. The parents of the boy call on the girl's parents or send a messenger or letter. Their proposal is usually phrased that they would like to become the "in-laws" *(bésan)* of the girl's parents.

The courtship negotiations can be conducted on such a highly formalized, refined, intricate level, but they can also be carried on in a simple, straightforward manner if all concerned are old friends and relatives. The formal pattern is more commonly found among *prijaji*, the urban upper class; the casual pattern is usual among village peasant groups and the urban lower classes. As an example of the informal pattern, a village girl described the arrangements for her younger brother's marriage: Her family was poor but respected in the village, and the young man had no property to bring to a wife. However, a village official with some land and an only daughter approached the boy's mother, and, with a protective cover of joking, suggested that the two be married. The mother responded favorably, but maintained the facade of humor, for both sides were afraid of rebuff. It would have been impossible for the boy's side to initiate such a marriage because of his poverty. After the wedding, the young man moved into his father-in-law's house and tilled his land for him.

A man may make his marriage arrangements himself without his family having any part in them. One informant, an old policeman's wife, said that her father was a villager who ran a food stand selling food and drinks where she worked and where her future husband saw her, with the result that he asked her parents for her. They brought her to him as soon as she had her first menses. The only contact her parents had with the young man's parents was by letter, since he came from a city a hundred miles away. She herself did not meet her husband's relatives until after the marriage, when, after the customary period of living in her mother's house, the couple went to her husband's home city for a short stay at his mother's house.

The engagement period is usually brief, sometimes as short as a day or two, rarely more than a month. Customarily, once the agreement is reached the man gives the girl a present, and later at the time of the marriage ceremony, he gives her another. These presents, even though they may pass from the man's parents to the girl's parents as representatives of the young couple, are neither bride-price nor dowry but tokens of the agreement reached.

The present or presents given before the wedding can be expensive or cheap, depending on the customs of the social group within which the couple move. Traditionally, a very expensive present of several cows or pieces of heavy furniture or the like was given about a week before the wedding. This was called the *sasrahan*,[5] which means literally "that which is handed over" and was not usually returned if the marriage did not last. Such an expensive present is rarely given nowadays except by a few rich village people.

In Modjokuto the most common engagement present was a few complete sets of clothes for the bride, including, if the fam-

---

5. There is considerable local variation in the terminology and customs connected with these engagement presents. The term *sasrahan* is also occasionally applied to the gift of kitchen utensils that the man gives the girl at the time of the wedding.

ilies were rich, jewelry. This was referred to as the *peningset,* which means "that which ties tightly together."

Wedding Rituals and Festivities

As soon as all parties are agreed about the marriage, the wedding can take place. There is no prescribed period of waiting; all that matters is that there be enough food and money for the celebration on hand and that an auspicious month and day be chosen. Once decided, the wedding is carried out without delay if it is at all possible, although often there may be a wait of several months until a harvest comes in.

There are three separate wedding ceremonies, all of which need not be performed. The one which is invariably carried out is the registration of the marriage at the office of the subdistrict religious officer (the *naib*) and his prayer over the bride and groom. This ceremony, although never omitted, is not considered the most significant by most Javanese. (The pious Moslems, *santri*, however, choose to emphasize this ritual and to de-emphasize the rest.) The second ritual, which is performed with almost as much regularity as the visit to the religious officer, is the religious meal *(slametan)* held at the home of the bride. At this small gathering of a few neighbors, the parents of the bride formally request the spirits of the house and village to permit the good health and welfare of the young couple. Most Javanese consider the most significant part of the wedding to be the "real" marriage which takes place in the third ritual, the "meeting" *(ketemuan)*. If there is no money available for a big celebration, or if the bride has been married before, this ceremony may be omitted, but if it is observed, it is the one upon which the most attention is lavished and the one celebrated with the most pleasure.

The "meeting" takes place at the home of the bride. Traditionally, she is considered not to have met her future husband yet and to be waiting at home for him to come to her. Many people arrange the registration at the *naib's* office, in such a way that the girl registers first and does not see the groom but returns to her home before he arrives. The home is decorated with flowers and colored paper, and an additional wing is built to shelter the numerous guests and the entertainment—a shadow play and *gamelan* orchestra, a modern dance band or an Arabic-style band, or a modern stage play.

The groom comes to the bride's house on foot, accompanied only by young men friends. His parents cannot come to any part of the wedding ritual. The bride stands in the doorway surrounded by her kinsmen and neighbors, literally supporting her on all sides; and the groom, too, is given physical support by his friends, at the moment of meeting. The impression is given that both must be helped through this moment of emotional confusion. Heads bowed and eyes cast down, the couple are brought near each other, and their hands outstretched to touch each other briefly.

The ritual actions which follow carry forward the theme of their meeting and their future conjugal unity. Bride and groom exchange symbolically flowering artificial potted plants, stand together on an oxen's yoke, and eat together from the same bowl.

They also sip water from a dipper offered by the bride's mother. Since at everyday crises in her child's life the mother's first act is always to give the child the breast, or, if older, a cup of water, at this crisis she offers a drink to her child and symbolically includes the groom. The theme of nurturance is sometimes again expressed at this same time, when a shawl (*sléndang*) of the type that a mother uses to carry her baby until it can walk is circled around the mother, bride, and groom as if she were cradling (*nggéndong*) both of them in the shawl.

Except for these two minor gestures, the entire focus of the ritual itself is on the couple and their coming together. One sequence, the washing of the groom's feet by the bride, acts out her subservience to him; but such subservience is, in fact, no more than a verbal ideal even among those who include performance of the ritual in the marriage ceremonies, and many consciously reject it as not in keeping with their actual conception of the married couple as equals.

The moment of drama over, the bride and groom are led inside the house to a specially decorated bench, where they must sit immobile for the next three or four hours while the kinsmen and neighbors celebrate.

Seen from the point of view of the exercising and strengthening of social bonds, the festivities for weddings and for circumcisions are identical. Both follow the same pattern of elaborate feast, special hired entertainment, and gambling and small talk all night. The same people participate. Near kin bring food and money, the men also helping with the construction and decoration of a special extension *(tarub)* of the front roof to shield the guests from the sun and rain, while the women (especially those related to the women of the house) are working for days cooking in preparation. Near neighbors and distant kin contribute in lessening degrees in proportion to their distance from the host. A crowd (ranging from a hundred to two thousand) of acquaintances, usually from the same occupational group, come as guests, each bringing a standard sum of money *(buwuh)* to give the host, surreptitiously slipping it into his hand under cover of a handshake.

The social relationships most intimately affected by the wedding feast and celebration are not those of the bride and groom but those of the parents of the couple toward their kin, neighbors, and fellow members of their occupational groups. Since each child is entitled to such a celebration, a son a circumcision feast and a daughter a wedding feast, a couple with many children will have a whole series of these events, the first usually the biggest, all serving to integrate them ever more tightly into a wide web of precisely reciprocal obligations with both kinsmen and community members.

Thus, despite the prominent role of the child, the ones crucially concerned in such affairs are the parents. They are the ones who are "having" the affair. When speaking of a wedding or circumcision, people do not refer to the name of the bride or little boy, but use instead the name of the parent, saying, *Pak Ardjo duwé gawé* "Mr. Ardjo is giving a feast." Taken literally, *duwé gawé* would mean "to have work," but the phrase is not used for ordinary work and refers only to the giving of celebrations for a wedding or circumcision.

The object of the festivities—the newly-wed couple—partici-

pates minimally and passively. They do not help in the preparations. They are physically pushed and pulled and guided like a
puppet through a series of ritual acts, culminating in an ultimate
of passivity: sitting in state for hours without talking or moving,
forgotten while the company feasts, gambles, and is entertained.
Both the bridal couple and the newly circumcised boy must go
through this honored immobility, sitting on their special chair at
one side of the festive house.

The family of the groom has hardly any role in the wedding.
They do not attend any of the rituals, nor do they contribute to
the festivities. After the "meeting" the couple stays at the home
of the bride's parents for a month, receiving guests but never
going out of the house. This period of seclusion is usually cur-
tailed today, especially among townsmen, to five days; sometimes
it is disregarded. At the end of this time there is a small ritual
visit of the bride and groom to the home of the groom's parents.
Here they may be received with another celebration as big as
the first one, and more hour-long sitting, or (more often) there
is merely a simple religious meal *(slametan)*. (Traditionally, the
couple then stayed a second month in seclusion at the groom's
house, but this is no longer done.) The taking of the bride home
to the groom's house is called *ngunduh mantén*, "to pluck or
harvest the bride."

The giving of both circumcision and wedding feasts has a
most interesting connotation. Although giving them is ostensibly
a parental obligation to the child, they have a further and significant implication for the boy or girl. One of my informants,
a young woman from the class of small urban tradesmen in the
market, who was asked why people spend so lavishly on these
feasts, why they often go deeply in debt in order to entertain
their guests more spectacularly, said that the feast is given for
the benefit of the child without thought to profit or loss—but in
the future the child will feel some obligation to the parent; and,
since he will probably never be able to pay the parent back fully,
he will have to settle the debt by passing it on to his own child.
People who are childless "lose," she said, because they can't pass
on this moral "debt."

Divorce and Remarriage

In spite of all the delicate preliminary maneuvering, the gifts, the official recognition, the rituals, and the huge wedding feast and celebration, no one really expects that the young couple whose marriage has been entirely family-arranged will surely remain married. Nearly half of all Javanese marriages end in divorce,[6] and most of these divorces apparently occur among

Marriages and Divorces, 1953, Subdistrict Modjokuto
(from *Suara Rakjat*, Feb. 9, 1954)

MARRIAGES		DIVORCES	
Adult monogamous	1889	Adults	1118
Children	5	Children	2
Polygamous	45		1120
TOTAL MARRIAGES	1939	(less remarriages—rudjuk)	206
		TOTAL DIVORCES	914

Rates per 1000 population—Modjokuto and U.S.A. compared

	Marriage Rate	Divorce Rate
Modjokuto, 1953	22.76	10.73
U.S.A., 1950	11.1	2.6

(Modjokuto rate is based on estimated population of 85,120. Source for U.S.A.: National Office of Vital Statistics, "Summary of Marriage and Divorce Statistics, United States, 1951," *Vital Statistics—Special Reports, National Summaries,* Vol. 38, No. 5, April 30, 1954.)

Per Cent of Divorces to Marriages, Modjokuto (1926-1953)
(based on my computations from official records)

1926—73.1 per cent
1935—16.4 per cent
1943—45.0 per cent
1952—52.0 per cent
1953—47.2 per cent

arranged first marriages. A girl usually has only one expensive wedding, and it is normally only the first marriage which is entirely engineered by the parents and which may involve an expensive engagement present.

Moreover, the elaborate first wedding serves primarily the purposes of the parents, giving them an occasion to reaffirm their social status within the community. To a lesser degree it can also be a kind of celebration of the girl's formal entry into adulthood, after which she is relatively free to make her own decisions. Once married, she may, if she wishes, reject the first

---

6. The following statistics, which although based on official reports, are not fully dependable, give some idea of the divorce rate:

choice of her parents; and the process of withdrawing from one marriage and entering a new one is simple and easy.

The Javanese attitude toward the first marriage was expressed fairly clearly by one informant, Pak Wiro. He said that traditionally a man who had a daughter who was still a spinster at sixteen would be embarrassed to have such an old maid on his hands. It might be that the girl was afraid of marriage and that the parents had, so far, respected her fears; it might be simply that no one had been interested enough to ask for her hand. Whatever the cause, some parents feel that the best solution in such a situation is to find a man who will agree to enter into a temporary marriage with the girl, the understanding being that after a week or so he will divorce her. Once the girl is a divorcée, she can easily get a husband, for a man who would have hesitated to ask for her before, when it would have involved an elaborate first wedding, will not be so afraid now; and she herself will, through her initiation into marriage, have lost her timidity and be eager to marry again.

Pak Wiro pointed out that, in addition to removing the stigma of spinsterhood from the girl and relieving her parents of their embarrassment, a *pro forma* marriage often serves the social and monetary interests of the parents, since it enables them to hold an elaborate wedding feast at which they can hope to recover, from the gifts of money that they will receive, some of the money that they have donated in the past to neighbors who were giving feasts.

Pak Wiro also said that a townsman such as himself would not resort to a trumped-up marriage of this sort no matter how ashamed he felt at having a grown daughter who was still unwed. It appeared to me, however, that a number of the first marriages I witnessed in the town must have been arranged with the following thought in mind: if the marriage worked, so much the better; but even if it did not, at least the initiation of the girl had been accomplished.

If a Javanese girl became pregnant outside of marriage, the situation would be embarrassing to all concerned, but not irreparable; as long as she were married by the time the baby was born, there would not be much scandal. In such situations the father of the girl often has to pay a man to marry his daughter. If the girl has no father nearby, the village officials may exercise their power to compel a marriage. If a couple were discovered to be illicitly sleeping together, the neighbors would be enraged, and usually send a group of village officials, or more often a group of young men, to storm the house where the couple are and force them to marry then and there, divorcing their spouses if they are married. Such marriages under pressure, which are relatively common in rural areas,[7] and which occurred twice in the town during the time I was there, although not among upper-class people, are frequently followed by divorce.

The second and third attempts at marriage may not be any more carefully considered than the first. The girl may again acquiesce in a choice made by her parents; and even when she chooses for herself her selection is often the result of a sudden whim or a chance encounter. Once a girl has her first marriage behind her, she can be freer in her behavior than before, and therefore she has more opportunity to meet men informally on the street or in the market. For Javanese a casual meeting can rapidly lead to marriage; and it is not uncommon for a person to go through several marriages before settling down in a stable relationship. Although a majority probably do settle down eventually, there seem to be many who continue shifting marriage partners throughout their life, even after they have children, and a significant proportion of the children I knew had divorced parents.

It is easy to get a divorce in Java. Husband and wife usually notify the village religious official (the *modin*), who helps with weddings and divorces and conducts funerals. He then accompanies them to the Subdistrict Religious Official (the *naib*), who actually performs the marriages and divorces and keeps the records. With or without the wife's consent, the husband is granted a divorce simply on request, and the major function of the official is to record it and to supervise and enforce the support of the wife and children. The husband is responsible for his wife's support only for a period immediately after the separa-

---

7. Out of the 1,938 marriages listed for 1953 in Modjokuto, 70 were noted "because of fornication."

tion—three months and ten days, or three menstrual cycles (the *idah* period). During this time the woman may not remarry, and if she becomes pregnant within the period the child is the responsibility of the husband. He is required to contribute something to the support of his children while they are young and can be forced to do so by the officials if he is financially capable. Usually, if able, he gives over a piece of property—for instance, a piece of land—to the child at the time of divorce.

The divorce action is called *talak*. If the man regrets his decision and wants to take his wife back within the *idah* period, the pair simply return to the official and the divorce is canceled with no trouble. This remarriage is called *rudjuk*, and a couple are allowed two of them; after the third *talak*, they must stay divorced (unless the woman marries and divorces another man meanwhile, which can be arranged if remarriage is desired). *Rudjuk* remarriages do not occur frequently; in 1953 out of 1,120 divorces there were 206 *rudjuks*. A man may, if he insists, declare all three *talaks* at once, thus severing the marriage completely, but the religious officials try to prevent this from being done.

Most Javanese are unaware of the intricate legal technicalities of Islamic law and simply rely on the superior skill of the religious officials to find a way for them to attain their desired divorce. Most Javanese are also unaware of the fact that Islamic law, if strictly interpreted, tends to make extremely difficult a woman's divorcing her husband. They are aware that it is actually the man who obtains the divorce, but most women are sufficiently adept at persuading their husband to divorce them if they are tired of the marriage—most often by simply leaving him. If he refuses and she remains resolute in her desire to divorce, it is more difficult, but not impossible, for the wife, by legal action, to force him to divorce her. At the time of marriage the husband makes a statement that he will grant her a divorce if he does not fulfill certain stipulated requirements, and she must prove that he has not fulfilled them. (To provide for her support and not to leave her without word of his whereabouts, for over six months—two years if he goes overseas—are the major ones.) The district religious officer cannot handle these cases (called *taklèk*);

they must be sent to the next higher level, the religious court (*pengadilan agama*). In the Modjokuto area this court is held in Bragang, some fifteen miles away, but most women seemed to be able to get their divorce without going to this rather extreme measure; in 1953, only 58 women used this course. I knew of no woman in Modjokuto who was caught in an unbearable marriage against her will simply because the man refused to grant her a divorce.

The reasons for the high Javanese divorce rate involve other factors besides the manner of entering marriage; these will be discussed in the sections dealing with the husband and wife relationship.

The First Months of Marriage

If there is any single period critical to the success of a marriage in Java, it is the first months after the wedding.[8] The young couple, often unacquainted before the marriage, inexperienced in sex, and forced to make a rapid transition to adult life, experience considerable emotional strain. The process of becoming progressively more adjusted to each other is called becoming *atut*, which means "to go along together." The basic use of the word *atut* refers to sexual compatibility, but it also carries the connotation that the girl is willing to cook for and serve her husband and is not embarrassed to be seen with him. Since, in first marriages the man is usually more sexually experienced than the girl, who is often completely naive, it is usually the girl who finds the marriage unsatisfactory rather than the other way around.

The difficulty of emotional adjustment, especially for a very young girl married to a strange man, is recognized in the folk belief that during the first thirty-five days the couple are especially susceptible to attacks by evil spirits and for this reason should remain secluded in the house of the girl's mother. There

---

8. Of all the divorces occurring in the Subdistrict of Modjokuto from October 1952 to February 1954, 6 per cent were within one month of the marriage, another 18.5 per cent had occurred by the end of six months of marriage, and a cumulative total of 41.5 per cent were within one year of the wedding date.

is a folk story of a newly married pair in a village near Modjokuto. The bride was very young and hated the man to whom she had just been married, but he liked her. Before the thirty-five-day period was over, the man asked his bride to go with him to visit his parents, and while she went she wept the whole way. As they were crossing a certain bridge, an evil spirit was able to enter her because she was so emotionally upset, and she disappeared. The groom, too, vanished, and then two trees grew up, one on each side of the river, and henceforth the spring near there was called *Sumbermantèn*, "Spring of the Newly-Weds."

An informant, Juminah, described her own experience in the following way. She had menstruated only once before she was married. No one asked her whether she wanted to marry or not, or told her the plans; and until three days before the wedding she was still attending school in the third grade. The parents of the groom, a young apprentice carpenter, sent her three sets of clothes, the *peningset*, and her mother gave them to her to wear without telling her their significance. When she found out, she refused to wear them. There was a big wedding with a six-piece orchestra, but from the beginning she refused to serve food to her husband, to stay in the same room with him, or to sleep with him. Her father scolded her, and even hit her. She had been going to school every day on her bicycle, and the day after the wedding she started to go again. Her father did not like this and secretly damaged the bicycle so that she could not ride it. She missed one day of school, but the next day, determined to keep going, she walked the whole three miles to town. But her father meanwhile had been to see the teacher, and the teacher would not let her re-enter school. She was still unreconciled to the marriage, and every day her father scolded her. Her mother would have intervened on her behalf but was afraid of the father. Finally, without Juminah's knowing, her mother went to a magical curer *(dukun)*, and he gave her a charm *(mantra)* which she gave to Juminah in a glass of iced drink. After that, although Juminah did not know about the magic charm till a year later, she became more reconciled, and by two months after the wedding her rebellion was all over and she moved to the house her husband had ready for her. Twelve months after the wedding she gave birth to her first child. She remarked that if it had not been for her parents and the magic charm she would have divorced her husband that first month.

There was another girl who was twenty-one but still not yet married when a teacher who had visited her house several times asked her father if he could marry her. The father agreed, and there was a large elaborate wedding. Since the girl's family was from the tradesmen class but the teacher was a *prijaji*, an aristocrat, with the title of *Radèn*, the family was very pleased with the marriage. After the wedding, however, the girl's girl friends teased her about marrying such an old fellow (he was about thirty). She became ashamed and would not sleep in the same bed with him but went to sleep with her little sisters. The teacher was then ashamed and went to the bride's father and said that he was going home. The father advised him to be patient and wait. But after all, said my informant, he was a *prijaji* and a teacher, and he had already lowered himself to marry this girl; so he did not wait any longer, and they were divorced only two weeks after the wedding.

After the ritual period of seclusion, living arrangements are made entirely according to opportunity. Since a newly married couple, if very young, are still dependent on their parents, unless there is already an empty house on the parents' land they usually move in with one of the parents (whichever has room) for the first few years. No one builds a new house for a pair of newly-weds; the risk is too great that they will be divorced within the year. However, even if they live with parents, their food budget will usually be kept separate. At the time of marriage the groom presents his wife with a complete set of equipment for the kitchen, which is often also referred to as *sasrahan;* and, since he is earning money, he will want to maintain separate cooking, at least, from the parents.

After a year or so of marriage and after a child has been born, since the marriage then appears to be stable, an investment in a separate house can be made. By this time the husband will have saved some money. Usually it is at this point that the parents settle on their child some portion of the inheritance due him—a house or piece of house land or piece of rice land. If the parents are well off, they will give small presents to the young couple all through the preliminary period; but most parents cannot afford gifts, and most young couples make their own way.

6. THE STRUCTURE OF JAVANESE KINSHIP

In terms both of generalized values and the specific customs in which these values are institutionalized, the Javanese kinship system is clearly bilateral. This basic bilateral emphasis, as we have seen, appears in a number of different contexts: kinship terminology is absolutely symmetrical in regard to maternal and paternal kinsmen. Descent is reckoned equally through the father and the mother. Inherited property is divided equally among siblings of both sexes, and each child has claim to inherit property from both his mother and his father and their respective relatives. Residence at marriage is bilocal in the first year, or so, neolocal after that, with no specific customary preference for proximity to one set of parents. The net of obligations and invitations surrounding the feasting-complex spreads equally in both directions, toward the husband's relatives and toward the wife's.

There are, however, some faint, and structurally unimportant customs which stress paternal ties: First, the rule for division of commonly earned property at divorce into two parts for the man as against one for the wife; second, the rule for division of an estate into two shares for each of the sons as against one share for each daughter; third, the custom called *pantjer wali* of nominal guardianship of girls by their male agnatic kin; and fourth, the prohibition, also called *pantjer wali,* of marriage between paternal parallel cousins. It has been stressed that, with the exception of divorce settlement, these customs are seldom observed. Division of inheritance by the two-to-one rule is confined almost entirely to a small proportion of the strongly Islamic *santri* families, and even there is usually only practised in the division of rice fields. Guardianship of girls by agnatic kin is in actual practice a rarely exercised privilege, which in any case consists only of the right to arrange a marriage for a niece in the absence of the girl's father, step-father or foster-father.

The divorce settlement rule, the inheritance rule, and the guardianship custom, are all Islamic laws. These rules function mainly in authorizing alternate solutions to quarrels among kinsmen. Aside from those cases of their observance among *santri* families, they are followed only when greater substantive equity can be reached through them. For these reasons, these "patristic" customs are to be seen not as structural components of the Javanese kinship system but as elements in Javanese religion. Islam as a legal system has hardly touched Java; its presence in the areas of marriage, divorce and inheritance is due largely to the support given by the Dutch to Islamic religious officials in the courts, officials whose competence was limited however to the giving of advice, and to these three legal fields only. The custom of prohibition of marriage to a father's brother's daughter is not Islamic, but may best be regarded as a structurally insignificant folk-belief, possibly deriving by extension or generalization from the *pantjer wali* guardianship custom.

After bilaterality, the second important characteristic of the Javanese kinship system is the absence of extended kin groups and the structural autonomy of the nuclear family. From the point of view of the individual, his kinsmen form an interconnected network of persons branching out away from him through his father and mother and their parents. From the point of view of the outside observer, however, the Javanese kinship system consists of a latticework of relationships not so much between individuals, as between conjugal couples. For the strongest organizational emphasis is on the marital pair, the joint heads of the nuclear family. This conjugal, or nucleating, form of organization of kinship is, of course, characteristic of many bilateral systems, including that in the United States.

The structural importance of the conjugal couple in Java is none the less so because of the instability of marriage: high turnover in membership does not necessarily invalidate a statement that a social group is structurally significant. What is more important is the fact that, at any one moment, most adults in Java are married. And the fact that, despite the considerable strain between consanguineal and conjugal ties, most familial differences are resolved in favor of the conjugal tie. The Javanese

preference for avoidance of overt conflict by minimizing interaction between potentially opposing relatives further accentu-
ates the autonomy of the nuclear family.

Certain consanguineal ties, however, appear to be less threatening to conjugal peace than others. These are the wife's kin
ties, particularly those to her kinswomen. These are the people
with whom the most mutual aid is exchanged; these are the people
who are more often secondary members of the household; these
are the people whose children are taken into the household; these
are the people with whom the warmest relationships are maintained.

Thus, while primary structural emphasis is on the nuclear
family, there is a secondary, supplementary structure—that of the
network of ties between related women. This is a form of kinship organization which has been called "matrifocal."[9] The
nuclear family is given strong normative and institutional support, and there are no norms or customs which strengthen the
kin ties between women. Despite this, these ties are considerably
more solidary than other kin relationships in Java.

Matrifocal organization shows up most clearly in household
composition, in the alternate living arrangements which are
chosen, when, for some reason—death, divorce or illness, for
instance—the conjugal household form is not feasible. However,
household composition is only an external, i.e., easily verifiable
empirically, manifestation of general underlying patterns of
dominance and solidarity between kinsmen. By dominance is
meant patterns of authority and influence in the making of
familial decisions and in the control of deviant or lax behavior of
family members. By solidarity is meant affection and loyalty, as
evidenced, for instance, in frequent mutual aid and in high social
interaction.

There are two spheres of kinship to which the term matrifocal might be applied. The first is within the nuclear family
itself, that is the relationships of husband and wife and their
immature children. The second is the kindred, that is the network
of relatives that each ego has outside his nuclear family. For the

---

9. R. T. Smith, *The Negro Family in British Guiana*, London, 1956.

nuclear family to be matrifocal means that the woman has more authority, influence and responsibility than her husband, and at the same time receives more affection and loyalty. The concentration of both of these features on the female role leaves the male role relatively functionless in regard to the internal affairs of the nuclear family. In such circumstances it is unimportant whether or not the male role in the family is actually filled, or whether or not it is always occupied by the same man. For the kindred to be matrifocal means that the persons of greatest influence are women, and that the relationships of greatest solidarity are those between women, or those between persons linked by a woman. Correspondingly the relationships with the least amount of influence and solidarity are those between men or between persons related through men.

Matrifocality appears to be a characteristic mode of familial organization in a number of different societies, which have differing cultural traditions but all of which have kinship systems which are bilateral and nucleating.[10] The social and psychological circumstances which are associated with matrifocal family organization are complex and can be specified only by means of extended cross-cultural comparisons, a task beyond the reaches of the present study. A few preliminary remarks however can be made.

The analysis of matrifocality as a characteristic form of dominance and solidarity relationships within the nuclear family and within the wider kinship network—rather than as a characteristic form of household composition alone—directs our attention to the role structure of the family.

Dominance patterns, that is, patterns of power, authority and influence, are aspects of the more general distribution of responsibility among familial roles. To which role (e.g., father, mother, grandfather, etc.) the major responsibility for familial welfare is allocated, depends to a large extent on the nature of the various general societal role systems, particularly the occupational sys-

---

10. E.g. the West Indies (Smith, *op.cit.*), the Southern American Negro, (Frazier, E. F., *The Negro in the United States*, rev. ed., New York, 1957), and urban lower-class English (Young, M. and P. Willmott, *Family and Kinship in East London*, London, 1957).

tem and the stratification system, but also the political and religious systems. How important or unimportant the male adult is within his family is directly related to the degree to which these general societal systems rely on sex as a significant criterion for role-eligibility, i.e., the degree to which masculinity is a requirement for filling the roles in these systems. If the man is the family's sole representative in the occupational, stratification, political and religious systems, he then has major responsibility for familial relationships to the external social world, and his power, authority and influence over his family is correspondingly increased.

Conversely, the degree to which sex is *not* used as a distinguishing feature of role-eligibility in these systems, i.e., the extent to which women are the equals of men in gaining a living, in prestige, political power and religious participation, is inversely related to the importance of the man in the family. Consequently, in such societies, matrifocal family organization becomes possible.

In other words, in order for women to be heads of their households, they must be able to be economically independent; they must be permitted to play an occupational role. In most of the societies or segments of societies where matrifocality is present, this is so. In these societies the occupational opportunities of both men and women are limited, and furthermore, there is a generally insecure economic situation which makes a man's contribution to family finances unpredictable and unreliable.

Insofar as women are excluded from direct participation in the political affairs of the community, and in religious worship, insofar as they are considered legal and moral minors, the wife is dependent on her husband for access to those aspects of social life. However, in none of the societies in which matrifocality is reported are the women completely dependent on men in these matters.

Another function of the male role in regard to the family may be that of status or prestige attribution. If the stratification system of the society is such that the various status positions are held by men only, then a woman may also be dependent on her husband for social placement in the community. Of the societies examined, only two—the Negro villages of British Guiana and the American Negro of the rural South—are women the exact equal of men in this respect, for in both of these groups all members are at the bottom of the social stratification system with no possibility for upward mobility, because of their color.[11]

The interpenetration of societal roles—in the occupational system, political and religious system, and the stratification system—with familial roles accounts only for the dimension of dominance and responsibility within the family. It does not, however, explain the matrifocal patterns of solidarity, the stronger bonds of affection and loyalty between women and between persons related through women, and the corresponding weakness of these bonds between men. For this reason, I believe, such a role analysis, in itself, is insufficient to explain the matrifocal character of Javanese kinship. Solidary relationships between a mother and her children can be accounted for to some extent by the psychophysiological dependency of the infant, but this does not account for differential patterns of solidarity between siblings, for the absence of strong bonds between the father and his children, nor differential patterns between more distant relatives in these matrifocal systems. In the Javanese case, an important contributing factor to the whole matrifocal pattern is the personality make-up of the Javanese. The psychological tensions between man and wife, between adult brothers, and between father and son, are related to deep personality tendencies developed in the course of the experience of each Javanese growing up within his family.

In summary, the Javanese kinship system is bilateral and nucleating, with a secondary, supplementary matrifocal emphasis in the areas of dominance and solidarity among kinsmen. The system of kinship terminology is generational, but with certain minor peculiarities which multiply the number of rank distinctions which are made within each generation. It is a system which is structurally simple, flexible and stable.

---

11. This is the hypothesis suggested by Smith *(op. cit.)* to account for matrifocality. However, Smith's own materials suggest that stratification roles are not the crucial determining element in matrifocal family organization, since he shows that the small "middle-class" of Negro teachers and shopkeepers, who are capable of some upward mobility and hence are oriented toward different norms of behavior, nevertheless show indications of matrifocal family structure.

CHAPTER THREE

THE FUNCTIONING OF THE
JAVANESE KINSHIP SYSTEM

1. CUSTOMS OF PREGNANCY AND CHILDBIRTH

The Desire for Children

CHILDREN ARE much wanted and enjoyed. The value of children is expressed in practical terms: "When you are old, your children will care for you. Even if you are very rich, the kind of care your children give you cannot be bought." A woman with many children is envied; a barren woman is pitied.

A man and wife who are infertile will go great distances to consult curers *(ḍukun)* and, nowadays, doctors for advice and drugs. The curer can offer several different types of prescription: a special mixture of herbs in water which has had a magic spell said over it, to be drunk regularly; a special massaging of the abdomen in order to "put the organs in proper position", or a long psychotherapeutic talk, the burden of which is, "If you are calm and happy in your heart, you will have children." Since usually it is the woman who seeks cure, it is evident that the blame for childlessness is generally placed on the woman; however, several times I heard unkind gossips say that certain couples had no children because the man had contracted syphilis from frequenting prostitutes.

Abortion and Contraception

The same curer who can treat barrenness is also good at abortion and contraception. In general, the same three methods—drugs, spells, and massage—are used. To have an abortion (*digrogokaké,* literally, "to be made thinner") is considered a sin, especially after the first three months; before that time the fetus is considered not yet human, to be "no more alive than blood." In spite of the availability of these techniques, married women do not take recourse to abortion, and pregnant unmarried women apparently rarely do, for there are a number of social solutions (marriage in form only, giving the illegitimate child to a relative) that are much easier.

One curer differentiated between seeking permanent sterility (*dikantjing,* literally "to be locked") and taking contraceptive measures designed to space (*ngarangaké,* literally "to make rarer") pregnancies. One drug for permanent sterility is said to be made of the fruit of the teak tree and a piece of the vagina of a civet cat. This is made into a sort of pill and a spell is spoken over it, and then it is eaten in a banana.

One poor urban market woman whom I knew very well and who expressed a strong desire not to have any more children considered going to a curer, but her husband would not allow it. He said, "What if something went wrong and you became pregnant? You would be bound to have a miscarriage unless the same curer was there because only she would know the magic thing to do, and if she was dead already, you would be lost." His attitude toward contraception was the same as that of most men: if more children came, it would not matter, food would be found somewhere for them. But my informant was in earnest about not wanting a child. She was only twenty-six and had had six pregnancies, three of them resulting in miscarriages; she felt that more would damage her health and looks. She said that she had even been keeping her husband away from her at night and had told him she did not mind if he went to other women. But he could not, or would not, understand. He thought that she was being unfaithful to him, and their relations were becoming strained. She asked me if there was some sort of pill she could take in order to space out her children.

The several other women who asked me the same question were all of a Western-influenced, educated group with intense desires to advance the status of themselves and their children; they said that they wanted to have fewer children so that they could send them all off to school properly. One teacher with nine children confessed to me that after she had four she used to pray that that would be all, but she never attempted any practical measures.

I asked a number of devout Moslem men (*santri*) about the Islamic position in regard to birth control. They all agreed that the problem had hardly been raised in Java and that they each would wait to see what the scholars might say on the issue before they personally took a stand. Their usual reaction was slightly against it, feeling that it seemed like a sin against God. One erudite scholar said that since there were no Koranic passages specifically against birth control the scholars' decision would be based on an interpretation of more general directives in Islam.

Births are usually spaced to some extent, in any case, since there is a traditional abstinence from sexual intercourse during the first thirty-five days after birth, days in which mother and child are more or less secluded in the house. Some couples refrain from intercourse for the first seven months of the child's life in order to give it full chance to nurse. Thus it is common for women to have two babies every three years.

Customs and Taboos During Pregnancy

The first sign of pregnancy, say old Javanese women, is a sudden intense desire for extremely peppery food, especially the salad-like *rudjak*, the sauce of which is, to Westerners, pure fire. It is a sweeter beverage form of *rudjak* which is later served to neighbors and friends at the ritual meal celebrating the seventh month of the first pregnancy. Even those modern educated or religious people who deplore the animistic ritual meal observance will not omit the serving of *rudjak* at the seventh month, although they serve it casually as if it were simply an ordinary enjoyable drink. As soon as the baby is born, the mother may eat no more peppery food during the whole period that the baby is nursing lest the infant be "startled" by the strong taste. This is the only taboo that is observed by the modernists.

The craving for odd foods (*ngiḍam-iḍam kaworan*) continues through the pregnancy, and the husband is required, no matter how impossible the task is, to try to satisfy his wife's wishes. He is also expected to refrain from intercourse with his wife (though many do not), perhaps for the same reason that they should not have intercourse during menstruation, because indulgence will cause the baby to be deformed.

The husband is equally responsible with the wife in observing a series of taboos calculated to prevent two great dangers: that the birth will be difficult and that the baby will be born a monster. The mother should not eat certain things: sugar cane—because, if she does, at birth the baby will start to come out, stop, start again, stop, etc.; a fruit called *kepel*, which has seeds with lines running horizontally—because then the baby will be born sideways; eel—because the eel gives birth to young, they say, as humans do. She should not sit in front of an open door because if she does the baby will have a big mouth and make a lot of noise. It is extremely important for the husband not to kill or to wound any animals during this period because exactly the same wound will be visited on his child. To confirm this a story is told of a Dutch woman who had a child which was born with a harelip, and the husband remembered that while she was pregnant he had hunted and killed a wild boar by slashing it across the snout. One of the shadow play tales is about the birth of Ganesha, the god with the head of an elephant, whose mother was frightened by an elephant when pregnant.

If the husband should happen to kill an animal during this period, he can forestall the evil by shouting out, "*Njuwun sèwu amit-amit djabang baji!*" (A thousand pardons, infant child!") This phrase is often used in ordinary conversation by women even when they are not pregnant, as a sort of safeguard against future trouble; for instance, whenever one of my informants wanted to comment on the ugliness or stupidity of one of her friends' children, she prefaced the remark with a quick "*Djabang baji,*" with the same effect as the pious "Heaven forbid that it should happen to me!"

Until the fetus is seven months old, it is not yet fully formed and is particularly susceptible to entry by evil spirits. For this reason the mother is especially careful, particularly if this is her first pregnancy, to stay near home, and during the sunset hours to shut doors and windows and not go out of the house because this is when most of the spirits are abroad. Entry by a spirit could cause miscarriage or, later on, mysterious behavior of the baby and perhaps death in convulsions.

The series of ritual meals (*slametans*) for the first baby is perhaps the best safeguard against these dangers, but this is not felt to be enough, and everything a person does is viewed in the light of its possible consequences for the baby. Bu Ardjo, my landlady, warned me many times, "When you become pregnant, be very, very careful not to be angry or nasty to anyone, even if he is Chinese or a bicycle cab driver; just be pleasant all the time, otherwise your child will be affected," and she used the word *ditular,* which means to receive something by contagion, as a disease.

Traditional Childbirth Customs

Besides sharing in the pregnancy taboos, the husband shares some of the responsibility in the birth itself. The traditional family calls in a *ḍukun baji,* a midwife who has learned her knowledge of magic from some other old woman, often her mother or grandmother. She spreads a mat on the floor or on a wide bed-sized bench and seats the wife on it, and the husband sits behind the wife upon a little bench about six inches high, supporting her between his legs as she leans back, straining to "push" her baby out. The midwife meanwhile is saying the proper magical spells for the protection of the parturient woman and the baby and is firmly massaging the woman's legs, thighs, and abdomen. The husband takes a mouthful of certain special herbs prescribed by the midwife and chews them into a paste; while his wife is in labor he spits them onto her fontanel, giving her added magical protection. If the birth is difficult, the midwife can do little but continue the massage. One prescription is for the woman herself to chew a bit of young banana leaf, together with salt, into a paste, which is then drawn down her body from the center of her chest to the vagina. Another thing she can do is ask pardon of her husband, turning to him and saying, "*Njuwun lepat, mas.*" This begging the pardon of relatives in situations of extreme distress (also done after a death, for instance) has, I think, the purpose of restoring proper order to the relationship (on the chance that there are covert hostilities present); with peaceable social relationships restored it is thought that equilibrium and calmness of mind in facing pain will come.

After the baby is born, the husband has a final task, which only he may perform. (If he is not present at the birth, a substitution may be made, but it should be some near kin of the new mother and cannot be of the parental generation.) He must take the mat on which his wife has been lying (*kopohan*) to a river to wash off the blood. There he must burn some incense and some dry rice stalks, put a flower and lime mixture (*sekar borèh*) nearby, and say a special spell taught him by the midwife to the spirit (*baureksa*) of the river.

The mother has given birth to the child sitting up; and for the next thirty-five days she must remain in this sitting up position, called *sèndèn*, leaning against a specially built backrest, or surrounded by pillows borrowed from the neighbors, never lying down even to sleep. She should also, as soon as possible, get on her feet and move around. This is so that the blood will all flow out as fast as possible so that she will be clean again. On the day of the birth there is a ritual meal for the baby, the *babaran;* and, although the actual work of preparing it is usually done by the new mother's relatives—her mothers and sisters, generally—and close neighbors, she herself is expected to be up and politely receiving guests within a few hours of the birth. There begin five days and nights of continual entertaining, often with all-night card games, traditionally (though rarely today) with all-night poem-chanting, climaxed by the big *pasaran* ritual meal and entertainment on the fifth day. For many women this means severe strain and sickness, and occasionally it can be a cause of maternal death.

After the emergence of the infant, the midwife waits for the descent of the placenta before cutting the umbilical cord, for the placenta is the supernatural "younger brother" of the baby, which together with the spirit of the amniotic fluid—which, being released before the baby itself, is the "older brother"—will mysteriously guard the individual through his lifetime. These two spirits (called *kakang kawah*, "older brother amniotic fluid" and *adik ari-ari*, "younger brother placenta") are called upon frequently in spells and prayers. Cutting the child free of his "younger brother placenta" is a magically delicate task, performed only by the midwife, who has the special bamboo knife and knows the proper spell to make the knife cut clean and the wound heal quickly. She then rubs turmeric on the stub of the umbilical cord. The placenta she buries in a traditionally prescribed manner outside the door, mumbling another spell designed to make the burial permanent so that the power of the spirit of the after-birth will be kept under control and not cause sickness to the infant.

Traditional Treatment of Mother and Neonate

After this come bathing and massage of both infant and mother. The midwife comes every day for the first thirty-five days to continue the treatment. When she washes the baby, she murmurs a spell which, among other things, states that the baby is actually a heavenly spirit (*wida dari*), implying (or causing?) it to be beautiful and healthy, and in the name of Allah exorcising all mysterious baby illnesses. When she washes the mother, she calls on the guardian spirit of the village, the *danjang*, to witness that she is washing away the impure blood and is calling on her own supernatural siblings (*adik ari-ari* and *kakang kawah*) to protect her. The mother must bathe in a special manner, pouring the water over herself completely, head and all, keeping her eyes open and blowing air out of her mouth each time. This is called *adus wuwung*. If it is not performed properly, she may become sick.

The baby must be massaged twice a day during the first five days and optionally for the next thirty days. This is called *dadah*, and its purpose is to shape the body properly and to exercise it so that it is soft (*lemes*) and not stiff (*kaku*). The mother, too, is massaged, but not so frequently, and this is called *dadah walik*, "to massage back to the original state."

The Javanese have a highly developed secular lore of home remedies, and nearly every older person can prescribe for any sickness some concoction of the leaves, roots, and fruits of plants available in the gardens surrounding every house. Those ingredients that are not found there can be bought from the numerous "drug" stores run by Chinese, another people famous for their home and patent medicines. For every ill there is a salve or potion. In the market there is offered a choice of bitter liquids, drunk daily by men, women, and children for general good health. Cheap wines are sold, under the label of "medicine," for women who are barren, for impotence, for fatigue.

New mothers, too, take a glass of this wine each day if they can afford it. They also apply a series of salves: one for the abdomen (*tapel,* one recipe for which included lime juice, oil, and quicklime); one for all over the body (*bobok,* made of rice-flour paste and a root, *kentjur,* which gives a tingling sensation); and a sort of mud pack for the forehead (*pilisan,* prepared from a ready-made assortment of roots and herbs bought in the market). Two potions are swallowed: one is to make the mother feel good, "cool," and contains about twenty ingredients—including ginger, garlic, roses, sugar and pepper; the second is a similar drink to make her milk taste good and flow copiously. The baby, too, is salved morning and evening and then covered with white rice-flour powder, which gives him a rather gray look.

Modern Medically Trained Midwives

For people who live in the town proper there are several choices as to type of childbirth care, ranging from that of the traditional midwife, (*dukun baji*), whose methods have been described above, to that of a medically trained midwife (*bidan*), who will go to the patients' home or have the patient come to the midwife's home, which is often equipped for lying-in of two or three women at once, or to the hospital. There are three doctors in Modjokuto, but a doctor is not called unless there is a real emergency.

Going to a medically trained midwife is highly indicative of urbanism, employment by the government, and education. She is more than twice as expensive as the traditional midwife. She charges approximately 75 rupiah as against the traditional midwife's fee of about 40 rupiah, and her services cease within a week after the birth, after the beginning of the healing of the umbilical cord. Since even the most urbanized Javanese feel that massage is the answer to all ills and call in the traditional *dukun baji* to complete the month-long treatment of massages, the services of the medically trained midwife seem to the penny-counting person of small means a poor buy. More important, however, is the fact that the midwife is usually a respected member of the urban educated group, close to the top of the prestige ladder, and, as such, is to be kept at an uneasy, honorable distance by those who do not already identify with her group. They are "afraid" of her, they say—meaning that they are afraid of being awkward and unintentionally disrespectful in her presence. Also, and in a very real sense, they fear the impersonal world she stands for, represented by the hospital with which she is connected and to which she might send one—away from the comfort of relatives and home, possibly to be cut open and killed. The *dukun baji*, on the other hand, is a village woman just like everyone else, and a familiar figure who often comes to massage one when one is tired. (Many people who live in town consider themselves basically village people.)

Another aspect of the step that is taken by the person who goes to the medically trained midwife is that it suggests the abandonment of the traditional rituals surrounding the birth and the adoption of a "rational" point of view. It happens, through accident of colonial history, that most medically trained midwives are also Christian and so have little sympathy for such practices as the recitation of various spells that are an essential part of the traditional process. However, this is not a very compelling disadvantage, since the crucial parts of the ritual—the burial of the placenta (which is carried home from the hospital by the father) and the sequence of ritual meals—can be, and are, performed in any case. The medically trained midwife attempts to prevent the new mother from sleeping sitting up, but women have told me that they feel better in upright position and insist on sitting up as soon as the midwife leaves, even though almost fainting from the effort.

An important difference between the *ḍukun baji* and the medically trained midwife lies in their effect on the roles of other members of the family. When the *ḍukun baji* comes, the husband has an important, active role in the actual birth, and the girl's mother and other relatives are often right at hand. There may even be some older children watching. But the medically trained midwife shoos out all these "interferences," in effect robbing them of their sense of responsibility and participation.

2. INFANT CARE AND TRAINING

General Treatment of the Infant

The Javanese feel that a baby is extremely vulnerable, especially to sudden shock which can lead to sickness or death. For if the baby were suddenly or severely disturbed by a loud noise, rough handling, strong taste, or physical discomfort, he would be *kagèt*, "shocked, startled, upset," and his weak psychic defenses would fall and the evil spirits (*barang alus*), which hover constantly around the mother and child, could enter the infant and cause him to be ill. All the customs of infant care can be seen as attempts to ward off this danger.

The baby is handled in a relaxed, completely supportive, gentle, unemotional way. He is constantly in his mother's arms and lap when awake; if he is sound asleep and the mother must move around, she places him on a cushion of clean cloths, with pillows surrounding him so that he will not roll off the sleeping-bench. In town, at least, if left alone he is protected from insects by a wire frame about a foot high which is covered with mosquito netting. At the first cry, actually at the first sign of awaking, he is taken up, cleaned if necessary, and nursed. A cry-ing baby is rarely heard, mainly because no Javanese can bear to hear the sound without trying to do something about it no matter whose baby it is. One evening at a meeting of a religious society, when the women present heard a baby cry out briefly from a house nearby, they talked worriedly for some fifteen minutes about whose baby it was although all knew that there was no untended baby in the vicinity. I was sitting early one morning among a group of women who were lazily chatting and buying breakfast at a little stand by the road when the train pulled up to the platform which was nearby. In the crowd that got off was a woman with a six-months-old infant who burst into terrified wails when the train noisily started up again. At once all the women in the vicinity, and there were more than thirty here and there, were rigid with attention and called various bits of advice to the mother, telling her frantically to try to nurse him, to feed him a ricecake, to put water on his head, to joggle him. She tried all these, but the baby kept on shrieking and the women continued to watch intently. There was not a single woman on the road who was not compellingly concerned. Finally the mother left, going down the road toward the market, with the baby still screaming, and all the women watching till she was out of sight and hearing.

Swaddling

During the first month, when he is sleeping most of the time, twice a day the baby is bathed, massaged by the midwife, fed, and then wrapped in soft cloths which are wound around and around his body, forming a soft cocoon. This wrapping, which is called *gedong*, holds the baby's body straight, arms at his side, with the feet sticking out free. The swaddling is not tied; if the infant should kick he could begin to loosen it, and if he cries, it will be taken off. Since active babies who seem not to like the wrapping are not swaddled, many Javanese infants are never swaddled. Swaddled infants are wrapped for only a few hours each day—those hours right after his morning and afternoon baths. At night the swaddling is off, and the infant sleeps next to his mother, as he is to do for the greater part of his childhood.

He is soon given a little short shirt, which leaves his bottom free, and a knit cap to protect his head.

Carrying the Baby

The baby spends most of the time, especially after the first few months, cradled on his mother's hip as she walks here and there about her work. She carries him by means of a long, narrow shawl (*sléndang*) looped over one shoulder and down over the opposite hip, which gives a firm place for the baby to sit, conveniently adjacent to the breast. Although a mother may shift the baby around to the back when carrying him a long way, usually he is in front of the mother's body where she is in continual close touch with him, nursing him whenever he wants, feeding him tidbits, joggling him if he is fretful; and if he falls asleep the shawl gives him complete support.

Carrying a baby in a shawl is called *nggéndong;* and it is this action that is usually re-enacted as symbolic of the mother's total care—for instance, at the wedding ceremony or at the harvest when the first ears of rice are carried home in a *sléndang*. The *sléndang* represents complete security, and most infants under three seem to prefer to be carried rather than to be left to run around, often begging for it from their mother. When an infant or child is sick, even up to the age of six or eight, the mother takes him again in the shawl rather than leave him lying on the bed.

Nursing, Supplementary Feeding, and Weaning

Although the infant is given the breast whenever he appears hungry, and although the mother is bravely drinking bitter medicines to make her milk flow copiously (at the same time abstaining from water or tea until her parturition blood stops flowing), the mother's milk is not usually considered sufficient for the baby's needs, and he is given supplementary feedings of mashed banana and rice paste. Beginning on the second or third day if the baby is weakly, sometimes not until the fifth day if he is stronger, or among modern people not till the end of the first

month, he is fed (*didulang*) twice or three times a day. Soft
overcooked rice and very ripe banana are mixed together till
they form a smooth paste. Then the mother feeds the baby with
her fingers, gently offering the mash to his mouth. There is no
forcing; whatever the child refuses is simply wiped off his chin
and reoffered. Many children (I would guess about half) refuse
the pap entirely and are not pressed to eat until they are more
than a year old. Town people say that village people (who are
often considered almost less than human, uncultivated, uncon-
trolled, unreasonable) force their babies to eat and swaddle them
tightly and uncomfortably. I have no check on the statement;
its importance lies in the expression of the Javanese idea that
permissiveness and gentleness are civilized attributes.

Nursing continues until sometime after the first year, and
most mothers have their babies with them all the time, nursing
them on demand. The time of weaning is extremely variable, but
few babies are weaned before they can walk at least a little and
are fully accustomed to eating solid food. When asked, most
mothers say that they weaned their babies at a year old, meaning
the Javanese year of 420 days, or almost fourteen months. If a
careful census were taken (which would involve almost impossible verification difficulties), the modal time of weaning would
probably be about fourteen to eighteen months. However, if
there is no hindrance, such as the work of the mother or her
pregnancy with another child, she may continue nursing a child
for several years. A frequent cause of continued nursing is an
illness of the child at the time of weaning, as a result of which
the mother does not have the heart to force deprivation on the
child. For this reason two-year-olds are frequently seen still
nursing. A child in our house continued to suckle until he went
to school at the age of six or seven, and was teased by his class-
mates when he went home at recess to nurse.

The working women, the *bakuls*, who sell in the market,
nurse their babies almost on a schedule. If they have no woman
or young girl to help them at home, they take the baby to the
market with them and nurse him there, but if it is at all possible
they leave the child at home after he is several months old. During his mother's absence the baby is fed spoonfuls of tea with

sugar in it and the banana-rice mixture. She nurses him just before she leaves about six in the morning, has him brought to her in the market in the middle of the morning, and then nurses him again when she gets home in the early afternoon. All the time that she is at home, as well as at night, he is given the breast whenever he wants it. It is likely that all of the working mothers tend to wean their babies earlier than others; at any rate, there is strong pressure on them to do so.

One of the market peddler mothers, Juminah, expressed her attitudes on nursing when I asked her about resistances to weaning. She said that some children who are always carried around in a shawl and given the breast every time they indicate a desire for it may cry a good deal at weaning. Moreover, such children, she said—for instance, the only child of a couple who want children very much—grow up without any incentive to do anything; they won't get ahead in school and won't go to work because all they want to do is ask and receive from their parents; and sometimes eventually they go crazy. What she considered the best way (and what she did with her children and what her mother had done with her) is *takeran,* which means to measure out. She said that this is the custom among market women: to suckle the child in the morning before going to the market, then have the child brought to the market for a ten o'clock feeding, and then nurse the child again in the afternoon (one or two o'clock) and when she comes home from the market. She said that it makes the child strong to cry some when he wants to suckle, and that her mother often did that—an exception to the usual Javanese attitude.

But this same informant was rather ambivalent about weaning the child. One of her babies had died when about a year and a half old with symptoms of diarrhea and fever, and she felt the cause was that the baby had been "startled" (*kagèt*) by a too abrupt weaning. She said, "I should have been careful to see that it liked to eat before I weaned it, but I didn't; and besides that, when I stopped its suckling, I did it abruptly, and then within a week it was sick and died." The reason for stopping so suddenly, she said, was that she was working in the market.

The method of weaning varies from mother to mother, but

what is stressed by all is the importance of not causing the baby to be startled and of gradually accustoming him first to eating rice and drinking tea, then to going without nursing in the daytime (but letting him nurse any time during the night), and finally giving up the breast completely. The final break is usually accomplished by having the child sleep in another house—with his grandmother or aunt—for several nights. If this is not possible, sometimes the mother rubs a bitter substance on her breast.

What is considered the crucial act, however, is a little ritual meal performed by the *dukun baji* who was midwife at the child's birth and who has directed all the rest of the child's ritual meals. This is not, however, strictly a standard ritual meal since the only participants are the child, mother, and *dukun baji*. Other children are not permitted to watch, but the ritual is usually described to them. In a little basket made of leaves are placed cooked rice and a cooked egg. A tiny model water pitcher is filled with water. Then the *dukun* casts a spell over them which goes: "Infant child, beginning today, do not drink the milk of your mother, because Allah has ordained that you may have your mother's milk from the moment of your birth until your teeth appear. If you take too much of your mother's milk, your debt to her is too great." (A mother's nursing, as in her carrying of the child in the womb and giving birth to him, is seen as placing an unrepayable debt on the child's shoulders.) Another version of the weaning spell goes as follows: "Infant child, you are going to be weaned. Do not drink from your mother, drink from this water pitcher, and eat this food. From now on look for your grandmother [meaning the *dukun* herself], forget your mother; do not forget your food, forget your mother's milk. Love your grandmother, forget your mother." These instructions, which are mumbled at great speed, are not really addressed to the child himself, but to the magical guardian spirits of the child.

Watching the behavior of mothers and children, I got the impression that, although in most cases the weaning goes off as scheduled, the mother is actually ambivalent about denying her child what it demands, and if there is any difficulty—such as the child's sickness or unusual stubbornness—the mother will give in. I encountered several instances when the child complained so persistently after being deprived of the breast that within three days the grandmother persuaded the mother to revert to nursing again. Although, according to Javanese belief, if the mother becomes pregnant again her milk is no longer good for the baby, often when the children came close upon one another the older child is allowed to continue to nurse through the pregnancy and to suckle side by side with the younger one. This is thought to be bad because neither child gets enough to eat, but still some mothers continue to suckle both at once. Or, even if the weaning has been successful, after the new sibling is born the displaced child sees him suckling and asks to join in, and most mothers give in at least once in a while. One common solution is to give the child for a while to a grandmother, who lets the baby suckle on her dried-up breast; and I have seen these old women with red, inflamed nipples, unable to bring themselves to say no to their adored grandchild. Another solution that is tried in every stratum of town society is the bought "pacifier," a little rubber nipple hung around the neck, on which the child —two or three years old usually—sucks as he plays.

Eating

From the beginning of his life the baby is fed some kind of solid food, gradually working up to the standard rice diet of the Javanese. At first he is fed, usually in a casual way as he sits in his mother's shawl at her hip, eating at his own speed as he watches the rest of the world. Later, after he can walk and sit independently, he is sometimes left to feed himself. Many mothers continue to feed their children themselves until after they are five or six in order to keep the diet balanced by seeing to it that the child does not eat all of the minute quantity of protein (usually simply soy-bean cake) first and then not want to finish out the rice which is the main body of the meal. There is, however, little attempt to make a child eat anything he does not want to; and if, when he is older and, intent on playing, he skips a meal, it is not thought important. The child is fed whenever he asks for food—initiating an informal, irregular pattern of eating that is to continue throughout his life.

Food preparation and eating for most families are based on one major meal a day and a number of snacks at odd times. Since it takes several hours to prepare the major meal, the first food of the day is usually either leftovers from the night before or, more commonly among townspeople, a small breakfast of rice with a coconut or beansprout side dish bought from a peddler for a few cents. The main meal is sometimes eaten around noon immediately after it is prepared; it may be kept till evening to be eaten at sunset or just before going to bed. Since the Javanese prefer their food at room temperature, it is not difficult to keep food ready at all times for casual snacks. In most homes there is always some food set aside on a shelf, and anyone in the family who is hungry helps himself.

Family members rarely eat together or even at the same time. In some families the older children and the wife are required to wait until the father has eaten the main meal, and then they have their meal and his leftovers. But, since he is never made to wait if he is hungry, a young child spends most of his waking time nibbling on something. Either he is watching his mother cook and receiving tidbits from her, or he begs for a dime from her to buy some goodies from a huckster. One informant told me that his little nephew kept up a chorus of "*Njuwun djadjan! Njuwun djadjan!*" ("Please can I have some goodies!") from morning to night—and usually got what he asked for.

Since infants are thought not to like the very peppery spicing of adult food, the nursing mother uses no strong seasoning for fear the baby will be "startled" (*kagèt*) by it, and she only gradually introduces it again into her own diet. But by the time the child is running around, his curiosity and imitativeness often lead him to try the highly seasoned food, and some children by the age of three are eating with relish food that few Western palates could bear.

Politeness Training

While still being carried everywhere, not yet fully comprehending the actions and words of people around him, the baby begins to be taught politeness. As soon as he can hold food in his hand and reach for proffered goodies, he is systematically taught that only the right hand is proper for such uses. The child is carried on the left hip of the mother (in order to free *her* right hand for polite giving and receiving and eating), which means that his right hand and arm are pinned between his body and his mother's, and the natural gesture in this position is to reach for things with the free left hand. Each time he reaches with his left hand, the proffered object is withdrawn and the right hand is pulled out by his mother; the child's own spontaneous gesture is ignored, and the proper one made in its place by his mother with his own volitionless right hand.

The same kind of learning by being pushed and pulled through a simple pattern of motion occurs in the acquisition of the speech forms of respect. Of course the child learns to communicate with his mother in the same familiar form that she uses to him, but from the beginning of his attempts to talk there is a deliberate attempt to make him use the polite phrases to all others. Thus a child's first recognizable word is often *njuwun*, "I humbly beg for it"; and I have often seen children little more than a year old, barely able to stand, go through a polite bow and say an approximation of the high word for good-by (only approximately correct phonetically but with accurate intonation, intonation being all important in polite contexts). The mother simply keeps saying the proper term over and over for him, just as she keeps pulling out his right hand for him again and again until he learns to do it himself. Similarly, the mother always refers to various adults by the polite term that the child should use until he automatically falls into the pattern. Politeness learning is highly emphasized by the *prijaji* (people of aristocratic value orientation), and a *prijaji* child of five or six already has an extensive repertoire of graceful phrases and actions.

Learning to Walk

Learning to walk involves something of the same kind of learning, but it is more spontaneous. Until the child's muscles are developed enough for him to support himself erect he is not permitted to move about by himself. Since he is carried around everywhere on the hip of his mother or someone else, he gets no opportunity to crawl. In fact, he is not supposed to set foot on the ground at all until after the seventh month ritual, the *slametan pitonan.* As his muscles begin to develop he is dandled on his mother's or father's lap a good deal and given a chance to try to stand, but only when he can actually stand and squat and totter along by himself is he permitted any freedom. This aspect of the child's experience must be exceedingly important in view of the extent to which adult Javanese are concerned with bodily equilibrium and spatial orientation.

Toilet Training

Unlike weaning and politeness training, toilet training is a matter of little concern. Whenever the very young infant is not being carried he is placed on a folded rag, *popok*, which is removed when soiled. Beds are usually simply a bamboo slatted bench covered with a woven mat which can be washed off. Modern urban people who have beds with kapok mattresses cover them with a rubber sheet. If the child is being carried in a shawl, often the mother seems to know when the child is about to urinate and shifts him a little away from her body, without fuss or sudden movement, to let the urine fall to the floor. Since floors are of dirt or, often in town, of concrete, cleaning up is simple. If the urine should flow onto the mother's dress, which is made of heavy, water repellent *batik* cloth, she stands up unhurriedly and lets the urine roll off. Later when the child can stand by himself he soon learns to slip off his mother's lap and to crouch at her feet to excrete. Until he is three years old or so, he never wears clothes on the bottom part of his body, simply a little shirt to the waist. Later, when he wears trousers (girls' little dresses do not offer the same difficulty) he can talk, and he is told to ask his mother for help. Through the ages of five or six, sometimes older, a child is never told to go to the place by the river, or to the latrine, where adults excrete, unless accompanied, because these are places of great magical danger; but instead he stays close to the house, and his feces are swept away for him. If the child soils himself, he is immediately washed off with water brought from the well or river. As he grows older he is taught by instruction and example how to cleanse his anus after defecation with his left hand, and how he should never use his right for this purpose. This is the obverse of the polite use of the right hand for giving and receiving, which he learned in his mother's arms long before he could comprehend its significance.

Attitudes toward Infantile Sexuality

The child's genitals are treated in a similar uncomplicated way. A mother when nursing her little boy will often pat him gently on the penis, or, if she is bathing him, affectionately ruffle it. A baby's erection is received with pleasure and more ruffling. Little girls' genitals seem to receive less attention, yet even they get an occasional playful pinch. An infant's handling of the genitals receives no attention; but when a little boy receives trousers (at the age of about four or five) there begins a steady teasing to teach him modesty of dress, and girls receive this treatment even earlier. I observed no genital manipulation by children over five or so; and no sexual play between children.

The genitals are often thought of as a part-for-whole symbol of the child. A term of address that is affectionate and preferred as somewhat gentler than the personal name and less formal than the standard *nak*, meaning child, is *lé* for little boys, thought by Javanese to derive from the word *kontolé*, meaning penis, and *nḍuk* for little girls, thought to derive from a word meaning vagina.

Going to Sleep

Whenever the baby is fretful he is taken up in his mother's arms, supported by the shawl, and taken outside and gently rocked and bounced to quiet him. In this same way he is gradually put to sleep in the evening. Later, as he grows bigger, going to sleep is a pleasant time; his mother lies down with him on his mat and puts her arms about him, cuddling him till he is asleep.

This is called *dikuloni,* and I do not think there was one child in Modjokuto who was not put to sleep in this manner. Sometimes it is not the mother; sometimes it is an older sister or grandmother or his father, but always there is someone. If a child wants to stay up late there is usually no objection from the parents, and at the shadow plays the children sit all night in front of the screen, watching and napping alternately. On ordinary evenings the mother will simply ask the child if he wants to go to sleep and will keep asking him until he says yes. There is rarely a battle of wills; there is no direct opposition. If the child wants to stay up, he simply does; but eventually his mother's mild suggestions and his own fatigue overcome him. If the child gets out of hand and these quiet methods do not work, the mother may frighten him with talk of the bogey man he will see if he does not shut his eyes.

Javanese, whether children or adults, rarely sleep alone. Young children always sleep with their mother and usually with their father too. Older children often sleep on another sleeping bench or mat in the same or an adjoining room, together with neighbor children. Young adolescent boys may sleep in different homes with their close friends. (Adults appear to sleep exceedingly deeply but seem to need less sleep than Americans and can, without discomfort, sit up all night playing cards, catching up with irregular naps the next day.)

Obviously, the practice of children and adults sleeping together in one bed involves a good deal of physical intimacy. Many children know about menstruation in spite of the fact that there is some attempt to conceal it. But the facts of sexual intercourse seem to be successfully hidden, at least from the conscious awareness of children, in spite of the fact that it seems to be carried on in the same bed, or at least the same room, as the children. Although I asked several women about this, all denied remembering any of their parents' sexual activities and insisted that their children knew nothing about theirs. Specifically sexual matters are rarely discussed, and modesty of dress after the age of five or so is carefully observed, although there is no marked restraint in talking about more general physiological matters such as childbirth.

Ritual Protections

The Javanese see the course of development to maturity as a series of stages of steadily decreasing vulnerability to attack or entry by evil spirits. A person who is psychologically whole and strong can withstand their onslaught, but the defenses of an infant or child are still undeveloped. The fetus is said to be "meditating spiritual matters" (*tapa*, the withdrawal from the world of the mystic), fasting, and going without sleep within the cave of his mother's womb for nine months in preparation for his emergence into the disturbing world. While this is the period of highest vulnerability, especially the first seven months, the period immediately after birth is not much safer. The first five days, until the falling-off of the stump of the umbilical cord and the *pasaran* ritual meal, at which he is given a name, are the most dangerous. For the next thirty days thereafter the infant is kept in the house, especially at sunset, and various magical spirit deterrents, such as a very sharp knife, are kept by his side. The next recognized stage is marked by the seventh-month *slametan*, at which the child is allowed to touch the ground for the first time. Before this ritual he is too vulnerable to the spirits, which find it particularly easy to enter people through the feet.

What happens to a child when he is entered by an evil spirit is called *sawanèn*, and the symptoms range from nightmares and hysterical weeping to extreme lassitude and sickness, to convulsions—in short, any inexplicable childhood disease. Additional precaution against *sawanèn* is afforded by a salve made of crushed onion mixed with a coconut paste, which is applied on the fontanel (another extremely vulnerable port of entry for spirits) every day for the first thirty-five days after birth and whenever needed during the next six months. This salve is called *pupuk lempujang* ("herb salve") and is a frequent symbol for infancy. It appears, for instance, in the oft repeated rebuke to a disobedient child of any age, "*Kowé baji, durung ilang pupuk lumpujangmu, wani karo wong tuwamu!*"—"You infant, you still have your *pupuk lempujang*; how dare you oppose your elders!"

As the child grows older he becomes less vulnerable. One informant placed the turning point—beyond which mysterious attacks are no longer called *sawanèn*, which is used only of children, but by the various names (*kesétanan*, "attacked by devils," *kesurupan*, "entered by spirits," etc.) that are applied to adult abnormal conditions—at the time when the child first begins to lose his milk teeth. This period also more or less corresponds to a change in social status, at least for the little boys, who are thenceforth given greater freedom to run and play where they wish.

3. SOCIAL RELATIONSHIPS IN CHILDHOOD

Parents

The child before he is five or six is said to be *durung djawa*, which literally means "not yet Javanese." The same phrase is applied to mentally unbalanced persons and to adults who are not properly respectful to their elders, for instance a daughter-in-law who is rude to her parents-in-law. It implies a person who is not yet civilized, not yet able to control emotions in an adult manner, not yet able to speak with the proper respectful circumlocutions appropriate to different occasions. He is also said to be *durung ngerti*, "does not yet understand," and therefore it is thought that there is no point in forcing him to be what he is not or punishing him for incomprehensible faults. These two related notions, of being *djawa* and *ngerti* sum up for the Javanese their ideas of maturity and adult interpersonal relationships, and they are the key to the whole complex of such ideas that are communicated to the growing child. But in the first years of his life these criteria for judging behavior are held in abeyance.

During his first two years, until he has been weaned and can walk properly, his mother is the most significant person in his life. Her relationship to him is characterized by nurturance, unconditional emotional support, and love. The baby occupies the greater part of the mother's attention, and the youngest child until supplanted is almost always her favorite; if he is the last child, he will remain her favorite throughout life. The mother is completely dependable. If she must work during the child's infancy, she may leave the baby for a few hours in the hands of her sister or mother, who are equally solicitous of the child; but she always returns to take care of the child herself when she can. If there is a divorce, the mother keeps the children with her.

As has been mentioned, the mother seeks constantly to protect the child against the perils and upsets of life, to exclude startling or shocking experiences—such as strong-tasting foods (hence her refraining from eating peppery foods while nursing the baby) or anger (his own or anyone else's)—lest the resulting emotional upset cause sickness. In thunderstorms mothers hold their hands over their children's ears. Since frustration and disappointment are thought to bring about the state of startle (*kagèt*), there is a constant maternal endeavor either to give the child what he wants or to manipulate the situation by distracting his attention or concealing things so that he will not ask for them. Every effort is made to blunt the frustration that may be caused by weaning. (That the Javanese see weaning as a significant transition in the child's life is shown in the fact that they call a child in his second stage the *sapihan*, the "Weaned One.")

The other significant transition at this early age is that of learning to walk, which also is carefully supervised; and the accomplishment of weaning and walking brings about an important change in the child's life: he can now move independently of the mother and begin to have relationships with his father, his siblings, and any adult members of the household.

Up to this point, the father has had relatively little to do with the child. He may have taken a turn, once in a while, at carrying the child in the shawl in order to release the mother to do something else, but he has not been an important part of the child's world. During the period of weaning and learning to walk, however, the father begins to show an active interest in the child; and there begins to develop a bond of warmth and affection between them at this period. One often sees fathers playing with their young children, watching over them, feeding them, bathing them, cuddling them to sleep. A man may take his five-year-old boy visiting with him when he goes to call on his friends.

The father-child relationship at this time has a special intensity, for it is only during this period of the child's life lasting from about the end of his first year until he is about five years old that he is permitted to be close to the father. After that he may no longer play next to his father, or trail along with him on visits, but must respectfully stay away from him, and speak circumspectly and softly to him. The child's behavior in general seems to undergo a change, and the once spontaneous and laughing child adopts the docile, restrained, formal, controlled demeanor of his elders when the period of closeness to the father ends.

The relationship with the mother remains as strong and secure as before—and lasts throughout the individual's life. While mothers are described as "loving" (*trisna*) their children, fathers are expected only to "enjoy" (*seneng*) them. The mother is seen as a bulwark of strength and love to whom one can always turn. In contrast, the father is distant and must always be treated respectfully. It is the mother who instructs the child in social forms, who makes countless decisions for him, and who administers most punishments. The father is usually only a court of last appeal and a model for imitation. He is expected to be, above all, patient and dignified (*sabar*) with his wife and children: he should lead them with a gentle though firm hand, not interfering with their petty quarrels, but being always available to give solemn sanction to his wife's punishments of disobedient children. Only during the one early phase of the child's life is this aspect of the father's role set aside.

Siblings

Older siblings are instructed to take care of the small child and, if they are much older than he, will resemble a lesser edition of the parent in their behavior toward the child. Since so much care is taken to protect the youngest child against frustration, the older sibling is enlisted in the task and is constantly instructed to give in to the wishes of the younger one. If the older one refuses and there is a quarrel, the parents blame him. Even siblings only slightly older than the child are expected to surrender whatever they have to him, although the parents consciously recognize sibling rivalry and attempt to arrange matters so that everyone gets an equal share.

As soon as a child shows a degree of dependability and responsibility, he or she is given the task of watching over a younger child if by this time, there is still another baby in the household. Most sisters and brothers seem happily unconscious of any jealousies they may have of each other, and to feel a deep affection for their little charges. The relationship between older sister and younger brother is one of the most enduring ties among Javanese adults; the older sister, like the mother, is said to *trisna,* to have unconditional love for, her younger brother.

Relationships with Others

The first discrimination the infant makes among the people who make up his world is that between nurturant mother and non-nurturant others. It is not long before the non-nurturant others are in turn differentiated, the earliest and most important distinction during the entire childhood period being that between familiar people, the members of the household, and unfamiliar people. The significant lesson taught to the child is that unfamiliar people, who are lumped under the term *wong lija* ("other people"), are not to be trusted. The parents and others who take care of the child constantly emphasize the fearfulness of the unfamiliar in contrast to the warmth and safety of the inner circle of his family.

From the time that he is old enough to understand, one of their favorite ways of persuading the child to behave is to warn him that strangers will do him some terrible harm if he is not good. If he isn't quiet, the soldier will shoot him; if he doesn't go to sleep, the formless bogey man (*momok*) will get him; if he isn't nice, the Dutchman will give him an injection; if he goes outside the front door now, a non-existent dog out there will bite him. Such threatening is so consistent and continuous that most very young Javanese children are terrified of all strangers and burst into tears at their approach.

The ostensible advantage of the imaginary-threat method is

that the agency which administers sanctions is, seemingly, not the parent, but its effectiveness naturally wears off as the child becomes more sophisticated. When it must be replaced with direct punishing techniques, the parents not only apply more direct sanctions, actual scoldings, and physical punishment but also, more important, begin to instruct the child in certain norms of proper behavior in the presence of outsiders and in the presence of his father which operate to make the child obedient and self-controlled.

Javanese Conceptions of Maturity

Sometime after his fifth or sixth year the child becomes aware that his parents, especially his father, seem no longer to have the degree of permissive, indulgent warmth that he has been used to; instead, they increasingly expect him to be obedient, self-controlled, and polite. Before this time he has been considered *durung djawa*, "not yet Javanese"; now he is expected to start to learn to act as a Javanese ought, to learn the specific forms of maturity that the Javanese value. The transition is not abrupt, however; and the ways of behaving and feeling to which he has become accustomed during infancy and childhood are not abandoned completely, for they form a basic matrix into which the new patterns of behavior fit.

The age at which this period of the Javanese child's life starts varies with the particular family situation. An only child or the youngest child in a family is allowed to remain babyish much longer than one who has younger siblings. The relationship with a younger sibling is often the first context in the child's life in which he is explicitly taught (and expected to follow) the Javanese values for repression of one's own desires so as to avoid conflict with the wishes of others and not be acutely disappointed oneself. The Javanese themselves discuss this transition period in much the same way I have here. Several mothers of only children told me (albeit with affection and indulgence) that their child was unusually naughty and didn't have self-control or "know *isin*" (of which more below), and that they felt that this was expectable because he was an only child. Javanese folklore includes many stories of only children and youngest children who grow up spoiled and immature in their behavior.

Javanese conceptions of maturity are closely associated with their view of authority relationships and of the behavior and feelings conceived to be proper to such relationships. The important lesson the child must learn as part of his growing up is how and when to act respectfully; for there are those toward whom he must show respect, and there are those with whom he may act spontaneously or familiarly. He soon learns that older people must be respected, especially his father and other men relatives who, formerly indulgent and affectionate, now seem to withdraw and to expect a polite relationship which verges on avoidance.

The shift in the father's role from one of affection and warmth to one of distance and reserve, although it is only one step in the whole series of events by which the child learns the specific Javanese concepts of self-control and respect, is probably the most significant both because of the crucial place of the father in the child's emotional life and because this transition period occurs during the period of the oedipal crisis. But it would not have the impact it has if it were not presaged and followed up by other events in the child's life, or, perhaps more important, if it were not for the meaningful context of Javanese ideas and values in which the whole transition is set.

The Javanese Value of "Respect"

The central premise which I shall discuss here is the concept of "respect" itself, a notion so peculiarly Javanese that it cannot be easily translated. The words for respect (*urmat, adji*) have complex meanings which only slightly overlap with the American notion of "respect." First, the respectful action is not evoked by the individual himself but by his status—as father, headman of the village, or educated government official. Further, unlike some usages in the West, "respect" does not necessarily refer to an attitude toward a person superior in power: in the Javanese family the mother exerts the real authority, but the father receives the "respect." A further difference from Western ideas of respect is that, for the Javanese, it does not matter whether a person actually "feels" respectful "inside" or merely acts as if he did. In fact, a significant aspect of all Javanese social realtionships is that the important thing is not the sincerity of the action but the successful concealment of all dissonant aspects of the relationship. And, although in many social interactions both sides are well aware that the true situation between them is not as it appears on the surface, all are happy as long as the superficial accord is not disturbed.

It does not follow that there is no emotional aspect to Javanese respectful behavior; on the contrary, there may be a very acutely felt emotional accompaniment, a component of "respect" signified by the three Javanese words, *wedi, isin,* and *sungkan,* which denote three states of feeling that are considered appropriate to situations demanding respectful behavior. The three words form a sort of continuum of intensity and specificity, ranging from *wedi* which is most intense and diffuse, to *sungkan* which is least intense and specific.

Wedi means "afraid" in both the physical sense and in the social sense of apprehension of unpleasant consequences of an action. Sometimes children when approached by me, a strange white woman, would tremble on the verge of nervous tears, and the mother would say, *"Adja wedi, gak ènèk apa-apa"*—"Don't be afraid, it is nothing." Informants, asked to give examples of the meaning of *wedi,* replied: "If I have to go out to the toilet at night, I am *wedi* of spirits"; "A child who is punished by his father is *wedi* to be naughty after that"; "My grandmother tells me all children should be *wedi* of their elders; if they don't obey them, they are not *wedi* of them"; "If I borrow some rice from a neighbor and can't pay it back, I feel *wedi* of that neighbor."

Isin may be translated as "shame, shyness, embarrassment, guilt." A child even as young as three begins to *ngerti isin,* to "know *isin,*" which is thought to be the first step toward growing up; and when there are guests children usually withdraw into themselves with an intensely felt sense of shyness and become completely unresponsive. A good example of this feeling was described by an informant: "For instance, you are taken visiting with your grandmother, and they ask you to sit down, and you say, 'I don't want to,' and they say, 'Go and play with the other children,' and you say, 'I don't want to.' You just want to be left alone." The child just stands there or buries his head in his mother's skirts, paralyzed with shame. This mode of dealing with difficult situations by inaction (as opposed, for instance, to the common American solution of increased activity) is evident in other contexts of Javanese life also—for instance, in the handling of quarrels, discussed later.

Other illustrations of the meaning of *isin* from other informants are: "If you are seen through the doorway without any clothes on, you feel *isin*"; "If you take something that belongs to someone else and he finds out, you feel *isin*"; "If you sleep with another man and your husband finds out, you feel *isin*"; "If you borrow some money and you can't pay it back, you feel *isin* and hide from your creditor when he goes by"; "If you ask to borrow something from someone and he refuses, you feel *isin*"; "If a village woman comes calling at her child's teacher's house, she feels *isin* and doesn't say much or accept anything to eat." A prominent clubwoman gave me this revealing example: "For instance, if there is a club and I have a position in the club lower than anyone else, I feel *isin*."

As can be seen by a comparison of the above examples, *isin* and *wedi* are by no means the same in meaning, yet there is an appreciable overlap. *Wedi* is a fear response, especially to strange things; *isin* is a complex anxiety reaction, involving not only fear but also a lowered self-esteem, and it concerns only social anxieties, most usually those having to do with social distance, including distance self-imposed through social transgression. While *wedi* may be a reaction to threats arising from the same kinds of social situations, it can also refer to simple physical threats. It should be noted that the discussion of *isin* and *wedi* here does not concern inferred commonalities of emotional response among the Javanese (although there are implications in this direction) but rather describes some categories of Javanese thought concerning emotional states, in this case those emotional states involved in the problem of social control.

Javanese children are *taught* how and when to be *wedi* and *isin;* they are praised for being *wedi* to their elders and *isin* to their betters. They learn *wedi* first, before they are capable of the differentiated internal response that "self-esteem" implies and the differentiated cognition of social differences. As they grow older, *isin* is taught them, first by mobilizing the already established *wedi* reactions, later by playing on developing self-esteem by deliberate shaming. The two-year-old, silent in fear that the strange visiting man will, as his mother had warned, bite him if he makes a noise, is not unrelated to the four-year-old who, stiff with shyness, hides behind his mother, or the adult villager who, when calling on a government official, hides not only his shame but also his purpose in coming behind a screen of polite sentences.

Isin is not supposed to be felt among members of the family, and it is thought to be a good thing if close neighbors can be without *isin-isinan* (mutual *isin*), going in and out of each other's house and borrowing freely, although most neighbor relationships I have observed were colored by a marked air of circumspection, insurance against unknowing transgression. There is never *isin* between mother and child; one of the common examples given for the meaning of *trisna* (unconditional love) is that if the person you *trisna* is wrong, you will tell him so ("Don't behave like that"), an action possible only if there is no expectation of an *isin* reaction on the part of the criticized person. As children grow up, however, they often develop feelings of *isin* toward their father or older siblings.

The result of the inculcation of *isin* in children is that at any formal public occasion, such as a wedding or a club meeting, they are exceedingly quiet and well-behaved and will sit docilely at their parent's side through hours and hours of formal speeches. If they become restless, which is rare, a mere glance in their direction by the parent is enough to subdue them.

The child begins to learn *isin* even during early childhood, and he develops and elaborates the feeling and comprehension of the contexts in which it is applicable after he is five or so. As he becomes more adept at social intercourse and, entering adolescence, begins to be treated as a full-fledged member of society, he learns the feeling of *sungkan*, last of the three respect concepts of the Javanese.

Isin and *wedi*, although complex, are close enough to American ideas to be translated "shame" and "fear," but *sungkan* is peculiarly Javanese. Roughly, *sungkan* refers to a feeling of respectful politeness before a superior or an unfamiliar equal. "*Sungkan* is like *isin* only 'lighter.' " "*Sungkan* is like *isin*, only without the feeling of doing something wrong." "If a delegation of official visitors comes to my house and they sit at my table, I sit off in a chair in the corner; that's *sungkan*." "If a guest comes to my house and I give him dinner, I say, '*Sampun sungkan-sungkan*' ['Don't be *sungkan*'], meaning 'Don't stand on ceremony, eat a lot as if you were in your own home' "—because the respectful thing to do is eat only one or two mouthfuls. Some village people are confused about the meaning of *sungkan;* they think it identical with *isin* but simply a more refined synonym, and they associate it with the world of *prijaji* values and ranks, where the ritual of politeness is practiced with subtlety and sensitivity. To know *isin* is simply to know the basic social proprieties of self-control and avoidance of disapproval, whereas to know *sungkan* is to be able to perform the social minuet with grace.

Teaching and Enforcing Mature Behavior

The nature of discipline and the canons of obedience thus change as the child grows. In the beginning, when he has just learned to walk and talk and has not yet learned either the highly valued respect for the parents or the intense shame feeling of *isin*, it is unimportant to attempt to persuade the child to follow anything other than his own impulses; and the problem, as Javanese parents see it, is mainly to structure affairs so as to minimize the emergence of impulses disruptive of social life. Keeping the child fed, clean, and amused is the main task during his first years. During this period, there are three techniques of controlling the child's behavior: distracting him from an undesirable goal, detailed unemotional instructions unaccompanied by threats of punishment, and frightening him with threats of horrible fates at the hands of outsiders or spirits. Actual punishment by the family members themselves is rare, and threats of withdrawal of love are never employed. No demands are made on the child until he is considered old enough to comprehend verbal instructions. These are delivered as a steady stream of calm comments from the adults to the child: "Go around back of the house to urinate," "Fix your dress," "Don't run so fast," "Say 'thank you.'" The assumption seems to be that the child is completely without resources of his own with which to face his little everyday problems. If the child does not obey these instructions (and usually the Javanese children learn early that evasion is more effective than direct disobedience), the adult does not show anger but merely waits till another opportunity arises to teach the child. There is no attempt or desire to let the child develop initiative or independence. In this early period, the only technique which employs anxiety as a lever is the threatening with fearful outside dangers. This is *wedi* in the simplest physical sense.

The values surrounding the Javanese phrasing of obedience are inculcated gradually. As the child grows older he begins to find that the people around him are not responding as they used to, that his weeping goes ignored, and, further, that he is expected to obey the wishes of his parents and that if he does not, instead of letting it pass as they used to, they punish him. Punishment ranges from a threatening look or sharp remark to shaming in front of outsiders, from tiny, painful pinches or quick slaps to actual beating (extremely rare) or tying-up. Thus the second meaning of *wedi*, respect due to the parent because of her capacity to punish, is taught. Since the child has been accustomed from the first to a minimum of thinking for himself, and has already acquired a preference for passive adjustment of tensions, this stage of learning, combined as it is with parental consistency in demanding obedience, rarely results in direct opposition to the parent, and there is a minimal use of actual punishment. Javanese children are markedly well behaved, obedient, and quiet.

Correct behavior toward persons outside the circle of the immediate nuclear family is induced by means of shaming. The threat, "If you are not quiet, the strange man over there will be angry," changes to, "Aren't you ashamed to be noisy in front of that strange man?" The feeling of *isin*, at first disproportionately and paralyzingly great, now gradually becomes more and more appropriate in intensity, and the child becomes more and more able to cope with a variety of non-family social situations culminating in his mastery of *sungkan* and its associated behavior patterns of etiquette.

After about the sixth year, the child gradually begins to enter the world outside the intimacy of the nuclear family. In town, at least, almost all go to school to learn there proper respectful behavior toward the teacher. Little girls are introduced to the world of buying and selling, soon learn to do the whole family's daily shopping alone, and—if the mother sells in the market—may take over the mother's stand for short periods. Little boys are given freedom to run with their gang through the town, although village boys have some chores, such as care of the livestock; but the girls must stay at home and learn the responsibilities of homemaking. Many children are placed in other families during this period—out of necessity because of death or divorce of one or both parents, because someone (usually a sister of the mother) has asked for the child, or sometimes simply as a conscious educational technique. Pak Ardjo, urban laborer with an elementary-school education, said that he intended to send Sumardi, his youngest son, then aged twelve, off to school in Djakarta, the capital city, where he would live with his married brother, and to send his granddaughter Sujati to join her aunt in Surabaja. He explained that it was a good thing for children to go away from home because, when they were at home, they were careless in their studying. If their parents told them to work harder they wouldn't obey, he said, whereas they would obey someone else. He thought it would be good for his granddaughter to go to the aunt in Surabaja because the latter's husband was very strict with his niece; when she had been there once before, she had not been allowed to go to the front of the house and waste her time but had to stay out back and help with the cooking and washing clothes. Sujati's own mother did not trust her enough with the cooking and household duties; away from home she would get more experience. She did not like this treatment much, he added, but it was good for her. Before the war he had placed two of his children in the home of a teacher while they were going to the H.I.S. (Dutch-speaking school for Javanese government employees' children). The teacher's house was only a block away from their own house, but they learned good manners there.

Parental surrogates are said to have a feeling of *mesakaké* for the children even if they are their own nephews and nieces, which in many contexts could be translated "pity" but here is better rendered as "conditional love." The children always feel a little stiff with them, a relationship often expressed in their use of respect language (*krama*) instead of the natural familiar language (*ngoko*) they use with their own parents. Living with them is a good opportunity to learn the variations and nuances of behavior associated with the terms *wedi, isin,* and *sungkan,* obedience, shame, and respect.

Peer relationships are extended, too, as the child matures. Beginning even in childhood, boys and girls almost always play separately. Girls continue the habit of quiet solitary play—with dolls or with miniature market stands with wares cleverly made out of scraps. Boys go through fads: kite-flying, marbles, rounders (usually organized by the school), and an assortment of other games. Although some of the games are competitive in form, rules are vague and never argued about, and no one plays for keeps.

Fights between children are rare. Parents punish their own children if they fight, regardless of who is wrong; and they consider calling names particularly bad. Parents are afraid that the parents of the neighbor child will become angry, in turn, at them. A common way of handling quarrels, customary among both children and adults, is the *satru* pattern—not speaking to each other. Children may *satru* with their playmates for several days, adult sisters, for several years, and divorced couples or debtor and creditor *satru* for their entire lives. It is an excellent mechanism for the adjustment of hostility in a society that plays down violence and the expression of real feelings, since it allows for the avoidance of the outbreak of rage while still permitting significant expression of it. A *satru* relationship is almost institutionalized; such a quarrel is labeled as such and is respected by all in contact with the quarrelers.

Children of the civil servant class *(prijaji)* often get their freedom rather later than other children because their parents prohibit them from playing with neighbor children from whom they might learn bad manners. But eventually they are sent away to school, and here they have plenty of opportunity for making friends with other children.

In summary, then, to a Javanese, *isin* and *sungkan* represent civilized, mature inner states. A person who "knows" (and by this they mean something like "has internalized") these attitudes and "knows" when and where they are appropriate can be said to be *djawa*, "Javanese." Since they are attitudes not appropriate to one's relationships with those with whom one has close primary ties, with the single exception, to a degree, of the father, the learning of the *wedi, isin, sungkan* sequence represents both a gradual widening and differentiation of kinds of interpersonal relationships in the child's experience and the development of specialized kinds of emotional competence to deal with them. *Isin* and *sungkan* are feelings that belong to the outside world, the world of adults. It is primarily through the shift in the role of the father, and the opportunity it gives the child to first play a role appropriate to adults, and secondarily through the child's increasing contacts with adults outside the family that the Javanese child has his first extended and meaningful chance to make the transition to maturity—to a Javanese kind of maturity.

4. ADOLESCENCE

There is no change in the basic pattern of familial relationships as the child matures. He remains dependent on his parents or parent surrogates, usually until marriage, receiving from them the greater part of his support and a good deal of advice about his affairs. As the boy attains full stature he may start to earn money—by occasional farm work, as a laborer in a shop making cigarettes, as a ticket collector on one of the many jitneys which go in and out of Modjokuto every day, as apprentice to a tailor or carpenter, and this money he usually keeps for his own use. Boys who stay on in school are dependent longer and continue to have to ask their parents for all of their spending money. Girls rarely work except to help in the mother's business. Although they sometimes continue school, they usually remain at home, occupied with a continual round of domestic duties.

Those changes which do occur in the adolescent's social relationships are connected with reaching sexual maturity, although sex is rarely discussed openly or joked about or directly symbolized in any ritual. A girl's first menstruation is received without special note. Traditionally, she was then married as soon as possible, but now marriage may be put off a few years, usually because of school. There seems to be a general feeling that if a girl is left unmarried very long, she will yield to natural impulses and as a result, become pregnant, which is not so much immoral as it is simply undesirable and awkward because it is then difficult to marry her off and the father may have to pay the groom to marry her. Since there is no institutionalized way of controlling the girl other than by keeping a constant eye on her, the simplest solution is to find her a husband as soon as possible. One mother, shortly after an adulterous liaison of a neighbor had been much gossiped about all over town, hastily married off her fourteen-year-old daughter to an eighteen-year-old nephew who was boarding in her house while going to school. The little girl was still in the fourth grade, and both she and her husband were expected to continue school. Relationships were to go on the same, the pair not sleeping together, but the mother felt more secure.

Boys, on the other hand, are allowed complete freedom. By the time they are married they are expected to be sexually experienced. One informant said that she thought that boys usually received most of their early sexual experience with prostitutes in town, who are usually affiliated with the coffee shops along the streets. Another woman said, with no moral or emotional emphasis, that her son used to ask her for the door key some nights so that he could bring girls home with him after the family was asleep and send them off early before anyone was up.

Sex is evidently thought of as an impulse which cannot be inhibited if external restraints, such as lack of privacy or a watchful husband, are removed. Many times young Javanese students questioned us about American teen-age freedom, unable to comprehend our dancing and dating customs as anything but a prelude to sexual relations.

A girl enters adolescence with her first menstruation, a boy with his circumcision ceremony. Except among intensely Moslem *(santri)* groups, who try to persuade the boys to be circumcised as young as eight, most boys have the ceremony between the ages of ten and fourteen. Parents wait until the boy himself asks to be circumcised, that is, until he feels himself to be reaching puberty; and it is said that usually the boy asks because he has begun to feel ashamed *(isin)* before his peers. One boy wet his bed nightly until his circumcision at the age of twelve, whereupon he simply stopped; his mother guessed that he now felt himself to be adult and was ashamed to continue this childish habit.

Circumcision is only a boy's first step toward maturity, the period of irresponsibility continuing usually until after he is twenty. Since he cannot marry until he can support a wife, he continues to live at home even though he is working. Often during late adolescence, boys leave home, going to another town to work or attend school. In the pre-war days the *santri* religious schools *(pondok)*, where groups of two hundred or so boys lived together in dormitories supporting themselves by farm labor or minor crafts, were very popular, probably in part due to the conflict between the boy's wish for independence and his unwillingness yet to take on the responsibilities of a family.

In contrast to this, girls—who from childhood have been given serious responsibilities around the home—have a very short adolescence and, by the age of fifteen may already have a child. In spite of her early acquisition of a family of her own, the girl remains more dependent on her mother and father throughout her life than does her brother. Her mother is on hand for every birth or other crisis, giving her advice on everything from the children's sicknesses to financial problems. The couple may live for several years at her house, and, in any case, are not likely to move far away.

I have already noted that for many Javanese the first one or two marriages, whether there are children or not, end in divorce. The girl, on divorce, comes home to stay another year or so with her mother and father, thus reverting to her childhood dependency. A man rarely returns to his parents' house after divorce, and he usually remarries rather quickly.

There is apparently a marked feeling of restraint between father and son that makes it difficult for them to live together. From the latter part of childhood, the boy is expected to be especially respectful to the father, to avoid speaking to him unless necessary, and never to eat with him at the same table. Once I was sitting with Pak Ardjo, our landlord, on his front porch when his twenty-year-old son came in unexpectedly from a nearby city, after an absence of six months. The boy simply walked by us, with no greeting, into the living room, where he sat down. The children went happily to greet him, told their mother he had come, and brought him an iced drink. After half an hour or so of conversation about unrelated things, the father began to mention this son to me in a long monologue of mixed criticism and praise within the boy's hearing. This was the first sign he made that he had noticed the boy had come in. The boy stayed a whole weekend, and my notes are full of statements like "father in front room, son out back talking to mother," "father out back, son on front porch." I do not believe that they had a face-to-face conversation the whole time he was there.

A man who needs a young man to help him, whether in a business or in a rice field, is more likely to turn to a son-in-law than to one of his own sons. Adult brothers may feel rather awkward with one another and tend to avoid each other. A man of about thirty-five, temporarily separated from his wife and children because he was transferred from an office in one city to another, had a choice of staying with either his sister or his brother, both of whom are married and living in big enough houses for him. He chose to stay with his sister because, as his mother said, brothers feel stiff together, while a brother and sister feel comfortable and at ease with one another.

5. ADULTHOOD

Economic Co-operation between Husband and Wife

Javanese women sometimes jokingly remark that all they know about day in and day out is *lombok* and *tèmpé* (Spanish pepper and soybean cake, the two essential accompaniments of the Javanese meal), but actually there is little of the man's world that they cannot participate in and still less that they do not know about. In the rice-growing cycle, there are certain tasks traditionally performed by women. After the harvest, in which men rarely engage, the rice is brought home by the women; and frequently its disposal, including complex financial transactions, is also in their hands. The market is dominated by women, and even the rich successful wholesalers are as often women as men. Women own and dispose of property as freely and competently as men.

There are, of course, some tasks which women cannot or do not usually perform. They cannot plow; they cannot carry as heavy loads as men (although some women come close to it); they do not drive cars or bullock carts; they do not do heavy manual labor such as road work, carpentry, or bricklaying. Office work, too, is primarily in men's hands, a result of the fact that until recently far fewer girls than boys went to school. Those girls, usually from civil servant urban families, who today are achieving higher education find professional and governmental positions in the cities with ease, but in Modjokuto most literate women who work become teachers. Thus almost the entire bureaucratic structure, especially on the local level outside of Djakarta, is male. Moreover, since most Modjokuto women do not understand the Indonesian official language, a knowledge of which is essential for reception of the political education that is channeled down from the government and interested groups through the radio and political party meetings, most women are not very interested in or informed on political matters. But in the sphere of everyday life, of getting and spending, women hold their own.

Men, on the other hand, tend to be rather dependent—emotionally as well as practically—on women. Although a man can, when necessary, cook a simple meal or wash clothes or shop in the market, few men ever do. Moreover, men frequently express the belief that they are incapable of handling money carefully, whereas women are supposed to have thrift and foresight; for this reason most men give all or the greater part of their earnings to their wives and are forced to ask for spending money as they need it.

This contrast in conception of the self explains in part the fact that Javanese men rarely live alone, self-sufficient, whereas women frequently do. A man always needs someone to perform the household duties; a woman can do these herself in addition to doing her daily work. If a woman is working—especially if she has a small child—it is easier to have another woman, perhaps her sister or daughter, to help. But two men could never make such an arrangement work. Single men can attach themselves loosely to a household, take their meals in restaurants, wash some of their clothes themselves; but sooner or later they get married. There were several older spinsters in Modjokuto, but no older man who had never married.

A rather illuminating example of a common type of marital relationship concerning money was provided by Pak Wiro. Wiro was perhaps somewhat more ineffectual than most Javanese; he was amiable and passive and completely without open expression of aggressiveness. He was a government employee who, after more than thirty years of experience, had hardly advanced beyond his starting point, in spite of the fact that he had had an education and bore an aristocratic title. Before the war, he said, when he was working in another city, there was a good deal of gambling among the office workers, organized by Chinese. Wiro's friends tried to persuade him to take a fling, but he said no, he didn't have any money because he had to give his entire salary to his wife. Finally one friend said, "I will take you to a Chinese I know, and he will lend you the money to begin on," and Wiro was caught. In the beginning he won, but after some weeks he found himself 100 rupiah in debt, which was a great deal in those days. Characteristically, he did nothing; he simply stopped gambling and neither paid his debt nor told his wife, apparently hoping that everything would come out all right with no effort on his part. Soon enough the Chinese came calling on his wife—not just one, but five, each holding a fraction of the debt. Wiro's wife was confused and worried, but Wiro did not enlighten her much; he merely sat back and let her handle it. Being very much afraid that her husband would be arrested, she finally arranged to pay each of the five Chinese Rp. 5.00 a month, half to apply on the principal and half for interest. In order to get the money she went to work, cooking and selling rice snacks and also setting up a little cigarette-rolling shop in her house. Thus Pak Wiro, rather like a little boy in trouble going to his mother, delivered the problem into his wife's hands and then stood pat, with implicit faith that her strength of will would clear up everything.

Not every man relinquishes his independence so completely to his wife, but most Javanese rely on their wives' financial judgment rather than their own, feeling themselves freed of an unpleasant responsibility. One highly successful old trader who had pulled himself up from poverty to relative wealth through thrift and clever dealings said that, since his first wife had been unable to handle money, he took over the purse and doled out to her, little by little, what she needed. His second wife, on the other hand, was an excellent manager, and he let her handle all the finances completely, conferring with her only on major decisions.

Men who receive a regular salary are especially apt to turn the greater part of it over to their wives every month. Farmers, too, whose cash comes in either large quantities at the sale of a harvest or in small driblets as garden produce is sold in the market, let their wives decide how to budget. But tradesmen who buy and sell in the market or craftsmen, such as tailors and carpenters, who need a fund of fluid capital usually have more complicated arrangements with their wives. One young couple I knew well, Juminah and Karto, had such complex and intertangled finances that it was impossible to analyze the profits and costs in his carpentry shop, his inventory, the interest on their debts, the daily intake in her cigarette stand in the market, or the day-to-day food costs of their household. After a two-hour rush of clothes washing and cooking, she would go to the market each morning about seven and stay until noon or so. She would take whatever cash she had, give part of it to the cigarette wholesaler with whom she had a steady running debt, borrow some more cigarettes from him, and spend the rest on food for the family and for her husband's helpers in the carpentry shop, who were paid partly in cash and partly in meals. He, on the other hand, whenever he made a large sale, would reinvest part of the proceeds in wood and give her a large part to be saved in the form of a bracelet or necklace. Sometimes her debt with the cigarette wholesaler would get too big for her to handle and she would use some of her husband's profits to repay it. Once, unable to deliver a promised set of table and chairs, he gave the customer their own furniture without asking his wife; and when she discovered this, she went into a rage and nearly left him. She claimed that such unilateral action on his part was insulting to her position as copartner, and that he should have asked her about it—and all the neighbors and relatives supported her.

The dimension of responsibility for major decisions of household management ranges from dominance by the wife to a point of almost complete equality between husband and wife, with discussion over every major decision. Rarely is a Javanese wife completely under the shadow of her husband, but there are many husbands who have passively surrendered to their wives.

A woman can own in her own name property that was hers before the marriage or that was settled on her in inheritance from her kindred. Such property—a rice field, a house, jewelry, a horse cart, a supply of cloths for sale—may even be the principal source of family income, which, in turn, is hers to dispose of as she sees fit. The property of the man, too, from outside the marriage is strictly his own. However, all that either of the couple earns during the marriage, including produce from individually owned property, is the joint property of both of them, to be used for the welfare of both partners and their children. Thus equality of partnership is understood from the beginning of the marriage.

The round of domestic work is all in the hands of the wife. If she is employed away from home and there are small children, she will have a servant or a female relative to help her. Cooking for a family is a full day's work, a day that starts before five with polishing the rice for the day in the wooden rice block and stamper, continuing through hot hours of fanning charcoal braziers to cook the rice, and a trip to the market to get the other daily food. The main cooking is usually finished by noon. At some point in the morning the clothes are washed, and in the afternoon they must be ironed. Since few people have more than two or three changes of clothes, they usually do a wash every day. Afternoons are generally lazier, but often there are little tasks, such as shelling peanuts, to be done.

There still remains the sewing of the children's clothes and the women's blouses. Many urban people do not do this work for themselves, having them sewn by a seamstress or tailor, but a good proportion still sew their own. Men's shorts and trousers are bought ready-made or made to order by a tailor, and the tubular *sarung* for men and *djarit* for women that is wrapped around the body from the waist down needs no sewing. No weaving is done in the home. Care of the children is actually a full-time job, since the children are never left alone to play by themselves but are under continual close supervision. But as soon as little girls are nine or ten years old, they are useful nursemaids and take some of the load off the mother; they soon learn to do the marketing and the greater part of the cooking; and if a family has none in the right age group, one will be found, either from the kin-group pool or from the family of a lower class neighbor. Little servants, aged nine or ten, are cheap; they need be given only food, a bench to lie on, and a minute amount of spending money.

The husband has little to do with the household arrangements. If the wife has many children and no help, he may sometimes lend a hand with the washing or the marketing or watch one of the children, but usually when he is home he is lounging in the front room, talking with his friends or fondling his children. He spends a good many hours out of the house each day; or, if he works at home, as tailors do, he is preoccupied with his own work.

There are several different patterns of husband-wife economic co-operation.

The first, common only in the towns among government employees and others engaged in occupations which assure steady work for the man, is the pattern of husband working and wife at home. Women of this class, often completely inexperienced at any kind of remunerative work, usually have a servant to do many of the laborious daily tasks; and, since servants need full supervision, the wife is kept busy overseeing the household.

The second is the common pattern for farming families in which husband and wife work together. Here there is no sharp line between man's and woman's world, although usually the various tasks are traditionally set; the man, for example, does the plowing and the woman the weeding. The third is a situation where the husband does the major productive labor and his wife keeps up some minor occupation at home, such as raising chickens or sewing to order or selling tobacco to neighbors. The fourth is a situation in which husband and wife carry on two separate occupations, pooling their income. The husband, for instance, works as a coolie, carrying heavy loads, and the wife keeps a little coffee shop; or husband and wife may both be teachers in different schools. The fifth is a business partnership in which both husband and wife work together. Typical of such an arrangement is the sale of *batik* cloth, which requires both keeping a stall open in the market every day and periodic trips to distant cities to buy at wholesale. Either the wife or the husband can do either task.

Other household teams besides husband and wife engage in productive work. Often a son-in-law is incorporated into the household to work with the father-in-law in his fields or to sew ready-made trousers which the father-in-law sells in the market. Similarly, two women can share the work involved in selling *batik* cloth or running a coffee shop, and these will usually be two sisters or mother and daughter—rarely, if ever, a mother-in-law and daughter-in-law. Another kind of production team, found usually among the craftsmen, is based on the apprentice-master relationship. The apprentice is often a kinsman—a son, younger brother, cousin, nephew—or, rarely, a son-in-law. After the apprentice becomes skilled, he usually leaves to set up work for himself. With the occasional exception of the apprentice-master team, in such arrangements there is no pay for labor, and little concern with differential contribution. All share in the proceeds as members of the household, the distribution of goods within the family following a rough balance based on need. However, the father in the family traditionally receives better food and dresses better than the rest of the family. It is for him that the one piece of meat is saved; and in some families no one can eat the main meal until after the father has had his choice.

In general, then, husband and wife together are the nucleus of a living unit which is concerned not simply with the processing and distribution of consumption goods but also with the production of goods or services to secure income for the group; and the potential or actual participation of the wife in all aspects of this economic endeavor gives her a freedom and bargaining strength equal to that of her husband.

Sexual Rights of Spouses

Javanese attitudes toward sex tend to create constant mutual suspicion within the marriage relationship. Since sexual intercourse, in or outside of marriage, is not considered to have moral significance, marital fidelity is not a moral issue, and a person who commits adultery feels little guilt. Nevertheless, there is also always present in the Javanese marriage relationship the mutual acceptance of the fact that each marriage partner has the right of exclusive sexual access to the other. As a result, each partner is constantly on the watch to catch the other in a misstep, and both are also looking out for a chance for an illicit affair—although women are less likely either to have such a chance or to take advantage of it after they have children.

The relationship between Juminah and her husband Karto is typical. I have already noted that Juminah was married when she was fourteen and that only after the continued efforts of her mother and father and husband was the marriage finally consummated. When I knew her, it was twelve years and six pregnancies later, and she was still maried to the same man. One day early in our friendship, before she fully understood my purposes, she said that her husband was out "fooling around." I asked whether she was not jealous *(tjemburu)* when her husband went off without her, to which she answered no. Later on in the conversation, after she had begun to place me as a student of family life, she became interested in my project and said, "Oh, that's why you know what *tjemburu* means!" and went on to qualify her first polite answer. She said that she was not jealous of her husband when he went out only in the afternoon or if he stayed away no later than eight o'clock, but that if he was out after nine she always demanded an explanation. She said that if a man stays out till eleven, twelve, or one o'clock, there is no possible doubt that he has a mistress; that some women just bear it and say nothing, but, if the liaison becomes public, the wife must make the man choose between the mistress and herself. She went on to say that her husband also kept her under surveillance. She went to the market to sell every morning, but when she came home she had to stay home. He did not like her even to go chat with the neighbors or anywhere else in the afternoon; he just wanted her to sleep. Therefore, in the afternoon, when he went away, she had to stay at home. She could not go out alone at night at all; if she had an acceptable reason for going out—to go to the store or the like—she had to go with a girl friend. She said that when all these rules were obeyed there was no feeling of suspicion between them.

Some months later, when I had come to know Juminah very well, her confidences led me to believe that both her own and her husband's suspicious attitudes were justified. She said that usually adultery was the result of chance meetings between people who hardly know each other. There could be nothing, she explained, between herself and men whom she sees every day, acquaintances of her husband, with whom she often jokes and whom she invites into the house. But a casual meeting was another thing—and her description of such a meeting had a vividness evidently derived from personal experience. For instance, she said, she might be standing in the doorway of her house, and a man walks by whom she does not know. He looks at her out of the corner of his eye significantly, and if she smiles he will walk further on but soon turn around and come back and talk to her. If she frowns, he will keep on his way. Or, as happens frequently, when she is selling cigarettes in the market a man comes to her stand and jokes with her, asking in familiar *(ngoko)* language, "Does anyone own these cigarettes yet?" If she is interested in a flirtation she will answer, "Not yet," and continue to joke with him. After a while he may ask, "Do you want to or not?" If she says yes, he will say, "I'll meet you at such-and-such a corner in a few minutes. I'll go first and wait for you there." Juminah said that she had never given her husband actual grounds for jealousy. "But," she added, "I'd do it if I weren't afraid of being caught by him."

According to her account, she had discovered infidelity at least three times on the part of her husband and had gone home to her mother in fury, bringing her children with her; and each time her husband had come begging her to come back. On the first occasion, when she was still very young, the house next door to theirs was rented to a man who had a small cigarette-making shop, and one of the work girls there used to buy Juminah's husband breakfast and cigarettes. Juminah, still naive after two years of marriage, did not realize what was going on until a neighbor told her. Then she left in angry tears and did not come back to her husband for some seven months. Now she feels that it was not his fault; the woman had seduced him. (This belief, incidentally—that it is the woman who seduces, who is passionate—is a common Javanese attitude.)

Since Javanese living quarters are usually rather crowded, and any adulterous liaison is likely to involve a number of accomplices, there results a typical Javanese pattern for dealing with such deviance. Nearly everyone except the injured spouse knows about it, but no one cares enough to interfere and to risk the anger of all sides. Moreover, the wife herself may be aware of what is going on, but she does not have to act to protect her self-respect as long as it is not apparent to others that she knows.

Only when the affair becomes public knowledge should she force her husband either to divorce her or to give up the other woman.

Javanese women are generally more deeply committed than men to the social and economic welfare of the family and therefore rarely overstep the marital boundaries. They are tolerant of their husbands' irregularities because men are considered to be by nature irresponsible. Their sexual promiscuity is called being *nakal* (naughty), which is the same term applied to disobedient or unruly children, there being no connotation of adult misdemeanor; and they are expected to be *nakal* both during their bachelorhood and after marriage. When a woman is young, her injured pride makes her angry upon discovery of her husband's infidelity, but, as she grows older and there are children, she is more concerned with the loss of money that might otherwise be spent in the family's interests.

When a man keeps a woman in another house, giving her money for food and clothing, the kept woman is called a *selir*. She is usually from the lower classes, and is not derogated but rather admired by her neighbors because she is better off than they. A wife who is unable to force her husband to give up this kind of expensive pleasure may have to choose between leaving him and breaking up their family or simply ignoring it. Since upper class women, *prijaji*, have neither the occupational resources nor the lower expectations of living standards of poorer women, they are more likely to choose the latter course; and it is also the richer men who can afford to support two women and families. For these two reasons mistresses and plural wives are more prevalent among the well-to-do. A mistress has no legal rights.

Since, although polygyny is a symbol of high status for the man and nearly every man aspires to this condition, no Javanese woman wants to share her husband, polygyny is extremely rare. In 1953 only 2 per cent of the new marriage contracts in Modjokuto Subdistrict were polygynous. The very few happy polygynous families in Modjokuto are usually pointed out in amazement by ordinary women. One such family consisted of a prosperous butcher and three wives, all living in the same comfortable house, each wife sharing a part in his business: one selling in the market, one supervising distribution of the meat at the shop, and the other keeping house for the rest. There were no children, which possibly explains, in part, the butcher's progressive addition of wives. The first wife was in authority, and there were no quarrels among the wives. Other women who described the harmony *(rukun)* in which the family lived, explaining that the husband spent two consecutive nights with each wife, invariably remarked that they themselves would not stand for it. (The term that a woman uses to refer to her co-wife, *maru*, also means competitor.)

Most polygynous families are divided up into two households in order to avoid conflicts between the wives. In such situations each household is socially and economically separate, and each is no different from the standard minimally extended nuclear family of Modjokuto. Very frequently, a man who wants to take a second wife will do so secretly, setting her up in a house in another town, and hoping that his first wife will not discover, or choose to discover, the fact that she has a rival or that—when presented with the already accomplished deed—she will give her consent. Since the husband is required to have the express permission of the first wife before taking on a second, such a secret marriage is illegal; but religious officials can be lied to, or—in the case of prominent men—prevented from asking embarrassing questions by the respect due their high position.

An illuminating case involving such a secret polygynous marriage involved a brakeman on the railroad. He had been married for seventeen years when he secretly took a second wife. Some time after his second marriage the first wife found the certificate of marriage in his wallet. Typically, she turned to no one in her trouble, simply kept it to herself, worried over it for a day and a half, and then went to the religious officer and asked him for a divorce. He told her that she was entitled to one-third of all their property because after so long a marriage the property belonging solely to each of the couple had completely merged with the jointly owned property. When she came home and told her husband about all this, he looked over his outstanding debts, decided he could not afford to give her her third, that he really could not afford the second wife, and just gave up the project and divorced the second wife.

A number of Modjokuto divorces had similar histories, the typical pattern being that the husband, possibly tiring of his first wife, took on a second wife, hoping that somehow he could make a success of it, and the first wife, learning of the marriage, either made him choose between herself and the other woman or left him.

It is clear from the above illustrations that the conflict between a person's view of his spouse's behavior and that of his own inevitably makes for potentially unstable relationships between Javanese spouses. The fact that minute deviations of behavior can be interpreted as indications of infidelity—with realistic grounds—explains why informants, asked to give the meaning of *tjemburu* (jealousy-suspicion), would give examples that seemed to show an almost paranoid watchfulness between spouses. The wife of a teacher said that when his girl students were visiting him and they were laughing together in the front room, she always felt *tjemburu* and went out front to see what was going on. The same woman said that every time her husband went to a *tajuban* (a gay men's party with one woman, a professional dancer commonly a prostitute, who leads each of them in Javanese-type dancing, together with much drinking of Dutch gin) he had to ask her permission first and explain that it was simply from social obligation that he was going. A divorced woman said that her former husband was so jealous of her that when they went to have their picture taken he accused her of making eyes at the photographer and tore up all the pictures afterward. She finally left him because he was continually nagging her suspiciously, evidently for no reason.

Marital suspicion may diminish in the later years of marriage. As women become older and have children to care for, the husbands tend to become more sure of their wives, and the wives, in turn, grow to care less about their husbands' behavior. One older woman who had had fifteen children said that she did not care what her husband did as long as he gave her the major portion of his salary every month.

Emotional Relationships between Spouses

Juminah, whose relationship to her husband has been described in part in the preceding section, one day spontaneously summarized her feelings toward him. She had been discussing the troubles her sister was having with her third husband—a weak man who, although he was faithful, gave such a large portion of his salary to his mother that his wife was deeply in debt to the Chinese rice merchant. Referring to her own difficulties, Juminah said, "If my husband does anything wrong again, I will ask for a divorce. This is better than loving him and his not responding, for then I might get sick and die. [Sickness is seen to be caused by mental suffering.] Even though I have children, I still feel this way. I can always get married again, and if no one will take me, I can go to work. [She already works daily, selling cigarettes in the market.] If you don't do something like that and just let your husband get away with it, things will just get worse later, and then you will come down with tuberculosis, and your mother will miss you when you are dead. Yes, I love my husband, and no, I don't. But if his behavior is bad I don't want to be told to love him. I love him, and I don't love him; that's the way I am. I love him with cautiousness. I just pretend to love him—that's the way it is."

Juminah expressed a number of typical Javanese attitudes. First, it is better to avoid emotional upset because sickness and possibly death will result. Second, it would be her mother who would mourn her death. Third, a woman alone can easily support herself and her children. And fourth, her "love" is a matter of external behavior and pretense (but, to the Javanese, "pretense"—*étok-étok*—is without any disvaluing connotations and is actually positively valued as a good way to deal with troublesome situations), and it is conditional on the behavior of her husband. This withholding of emotional commitment is apparently typical of most Javanese marriages.

One rather intellectually inclined, middle-aged *prijaji* office worker, Pak Wiro, whose monetary relationship with his wife was described some pages back, said, speaking rather impersonally about "the Javanese husband-and-wife relationship," that when the husband and wife are still young there are two main feelings: suspicion *(tjemburu)* and separateness. That is, he elaborated, when one of them is troubled or sick the other does not share the sorrow, does not worry. This separateness is very usual, he said, along with intense suspicion—husband and wife always suspect each other very much when still young—and he himself was like this when first married. If his wife was upset or sick, it made no difference to him; he just went off wherever he was going, and she did the same on her side when he was sick. Thus the relation between man and wife is one of mere liking *(remen)*, not yet love *(trisna)*, and watchfulness, he said. Some people never get past this period—particularly village people, Pak Wiro thought; but *prijajis*, or many of them, finally get to a point where the relation of man and wife is one of love. There is no longer suspicion between them, and if one is troubled the other is troubled too; this is the way he and his wife are now, he added. Pak Wiro had been married stably for twenty-five years despite the fact that he and his wife had never had children—although they brought up a series of nephews and nieces as their own.

Kardjo, urban laborer and laundryman in the Dutch hospital, also expressed some of the same attitudes. He had been married to only one woman and had some ten children, but nevertheless felt that a wife should be abandoned if she made any trouble for the husband. The conversation had been about his statement that several people in the neighborhood were 135 and 150 years old. When asked how it was that people could live so long he said that it was because their hearts were peaceful; they never got angry, never got upset about anything, and so they could live very long. When asked how one could become so peaceful, he said that he did not know—that if one is lucky, nothing very serious will happen to upset one. He said, "One thing that sometimes helps is that if you have a lot of wives you just keep changing them, and as soon as you start having trouble with one you leave and go marry another." I asked whether most Javanese thought this was a good thing—to marry and divorce frequently. He replied: "Yes, that is one way to avoid having trouble, you just leave it behind when you get divorced." He added that some people had more than one wife at a time. That was good, and he would like it, but the difficulty was that one had to support them all. One of the reasons we Javanese divorce our wives easily, he said, was that one does not have to provide anything for them after a divorce the way the Dutch do; one is no longer responsible for feeding, clothing, and housing them. He said also that other people do not think anything against people who get divorces.

The handling of quarrels between husband and wife also fits a general pattern. Anger is to be avoided if possible, and, above all, the neighbors must not know about any quarrel; they must not hear the sounds of quarreling. Some couples have never been seen to quarrel; some retire into the bedroom to whisper it out so that even their own children will not know they are fighting. Many husbands—perhaps most—give in to their wives most of the time in order to avoid unpleasantness, the rationale for such rather meek behavior being that men, since they are more spiritually advanced than women, should behave accordingly; that men are by nature more capable of being patient *(sabar)* than women, who are born impulsive. One woman said that she and her husband never fought (which was apparently true, at least for the period of more than a year during which we shared their house); that if he was angry she would retire to the back of the house and not listen to him, and if she was angry he would just leave the house for a while.

When such techniques of avoidance fail and tempers flare up, husband and wife usually do not speak to each other for a week or so, sending messages if necessary by way of their children. Nearly every couple interviewed said that this silent expression of hostility, called *satru*, was the usual form of their quarrels. A common method of settling differences is by appeal to a go-between. The husband may go to his wife's mother to persuade her to come to her senses, or the wife to one of the husband's relatives. The go-between pattern appears in other contexts in Javanese life, particularly in delicate matters such as arranging a loan or a marriage, and is part of a more pervasive pattern of general avoidance of direct contacts that are potentially explosive.

A strong positive tie between Javanese husband and wife is

exerted by the presence of children, especially as the marriage continues. I have described the intimate part the man has in each pregnancy and birth and in the early care of the child. A custom which emphasizes the tie through the child is that of teknonymy: the husband addresses his wife as "mother of Slamet" (*mbokné* Slamet) and the wife addresses her husband as "father of Slamet" (*pakné* Slamet); sometimes the terms are shortened to just "mother of it" (*mbokné*) and "father of it" (*pakné*). Other people, too, refer to them in the same way, sometimes to the extent that their original names are forgotten.

Aristocrats, *prijajis*, do not use this form of address. They, and other urban people who follow their usage, say "little sister" (*ḍik* or, in very polite circles, *djeng*) for "wife," and "older brother" (*mas, kangmas*) for "husband," the connotation being that the husband protects his wife as he does his little sister. Older *prijaji* couples may address each other in this way, or they may call each other "father" (*pak*) or "mother" (*bu*). A very old couple address each other as "grandparent" (*mbah*). By using such terms of kinship, husband and wife refer, especially when using teknonymy, to the consanguineal link between them through their child. Other kin may also use further extensions of teknonymy (*buḍéné* Slamet, "aunt of Slamet"; *mbakjuné* Slamet, "older sister of Slamet"), usually only in the presence of the child in order to teach him proper address terms, but sometimes with the conscious purpose of emphasizing a particular kin tie.

Divorce

The several different Javanese attitudes toward divorce seem to be associated with the various religious orientations present in Javanese culture.

The numerically largest group, those peasants and lower class town dwellers who emphasize the animistic elements in Javanese religion, and who tend to a sort of individualistic ethic, the *abangan*, see divorce entirely situationally—as neither good nor bad in itself, and regard it as a better solution to a conflict than the ever-present danger of sickness which is seen as a consequence of internal turmoil.

Another group, the *santris*, which includes peasants and lower- and middle-class town dwellers who emphasize orthodox Islamic teachings, consider divorce morally wrong. One informant, a young, serious, slightly educated *santri* peasant who had been married about a year, said: "People who know the [Moslem] law do not divorce; at any rate, they try very hard not to. If they are illiterate, they don't know any better and divorce easily. I am always careful not to cause a divorce. For this reason I speak to my wife as seldom as possible." When asked if he had ever quarreled with his wife to the point of their not speaking to each other *(satru)*, he said no, that was the same as divorce and to be avoided; if he was angry he kept it in and showed no sign of his anger. But *santris*, no less than *abangans*, have a high divorce rate, with the possible exception of the urban, sophisticated *santris*. It seems possible that the Islamic disvaluation of divorce is not sufficiently strong to counteract the influence of those aspects of the kinship and occupational systems, identical for both *santris* and *abangans*, that encourage easy divorce.

A third group, the *prijaji* townsmen, especially those in the governmental bureaucracy, who see themselves as members of an aristocracy and emphasize the Hindu-Buddhist aspects of Javanese religion, have a considerably lower divorce rate than the other groups. Of all the 180 members of the women's club *(Perwari)* in Modjokuto, to which nearly every *prijaji* matron belonged, there were only five women who had ever been divorced or whose husbands had ever been divorced, and—with the one exception of a prominent, much-marrying man who usually had several wives concurrently—none of these had ever been divorced more than once. *Prijajis* do not disapprove of divorce as such, but they deplore any action which reveals a person's inner self as lacking in refinement and control. This self-ideal is always seen by the *prijajis* as a contrast to their notion of the peasant as un- cultivated and driven by worldly desires. Thus the self-image is more than simply a personal measure; it is a major element in the social ranking of individuals, with which *prijajis*—even more than the mass of Javanese—are continually preoccupied. For a *prijaji*, then, it is a matter of shame and withdrawal of social esteem to be divorced, and as a result divorces among *prijajis* are rare.

One *prijaji* woman, Bu Rekso, when asked about this difference in divorce rate, said that she thought the reason was that *prijajis* are ashamed *(isin)* if people know about any behavior of theirs that isn't good. Village people, she said, don't feel *isin* about divorce; but a *prijaji* would never divorce any more than she would carry a basket on her back (which is the typical posture of peasant women carrying heavy loads of vegetables in the market).[1]

There is no single "causal factor" to explain the high Javanese divorce rate. Rather, one finds a set of conditions favorable to divorce no one of which is alone sufficient reason for divorce. We have seen that one of the most important structural reasons is the fact that the courtship period is extremely abbreviated and, in many cases, completely omitted; that, with the arrangement of the marriage by the parents, the young couple has little chance to know one another before the wedding, and that even after the first marriage, when the individual is more free to choose his own spouse, the choice is rarely given very serious thought. It would appear that, more often than not, a Javanese couple have the wedding first and then, in the months following, find out whether or not they will get along together.

The reasons given by divorcing couples themselves are illuminating; the one most often cited being sexual infidelity. One of the five *prijaji* divorces in Modjokuto was said to be due to the fact that the husband had been sleeping with his wife's niece, who was living with them. Some informants thought that the wife could have borne it emotionally, but that the husband's misconduct was so flagrant that she had to divorce him. Another

1. Bu Rekso, I may add, was married to a notoriously promiscuous man who, in addition to frequenting prostitutes, boasted to all the neighborhood men that he had three other wives, of whom this wife was unaware, scattered around the subdistrict. He was a man whom any *abangan* woman would have divorced long ago. Bu Rekso would never speak about the matter, behaving as if she knew nothing of it; but a projective test (T.A.T.) administered to her contained a repeated theme of women struggling to reach internal composure in the face of external conflicts, some of which concerned unfaithful husbands.

woman, now a seamstress supporting herself, said she divorced her husband because he was going every night to a nurse who lived nearby and that she herself saw them walking together. She could bear it in her external behavior, she said, but inwardly she was seething, "hot" *(panas)*, and demanded a divorce. In a third case, the ten-year-old son of a policeman told his mother that his father had asked to borrow his bike in order to take a girl friend riding. The mother then waited until her husband was on duty, sold all the furniture, took all the valuables, and went home with her son to her mother. In a fourth case of a rarer type in which the woman was at fault, the husband was a tailor who worked at home while the wife went every day to the market to sell onions. She fell in love with a man who sold onions next to her and abandoned her three children and husband to go live with him, in spite of scoldings by friends, neighbors, and religious officers, who were forced eventually to give her a divorce.

The second general reason given for divorce is economic irresponsibility. One young mother whose husband could not have been more than eighteen years old, and who left him to return to her own mother, said that the reason was that he would not save his money but went to the movies every night and spent it. One Modjokuto woman was married to a young clerk in the sugar factory near Modjokuto and had a baby by him and a little daughter by a previous marriage when the second wave of the Indonesian revolution swept over the Modjokuto area. The husband, frightened not only of the Dutch but also of the Indonesian soldiers as well because of his association with the factory, fled in terror, leaving her and the children to fend for themselves. She was equally terrified and went home to her mother, some five fearful miles away. Later, when her husband returned, she refused to rejoin him, claiming that he had unrightfully abandoned her.

A third case, which is cited here in some detail because it illustrates several typical features of Javanese kinship, concerns Pak Subroto, who had worked as a clerk for Dutch sugar factories for many years before the war. After one brief marriage which ended in divorce, he had married the daughter of a wealthy peasant and had five children by her. She died at the time of the birth of her last child. She had been given a good deal of land and a house by her parents, property which, since it was exclusively hers, not he but his children were eligible to inherit. Having no property of his own, he had found himself guardian of his children's property, and he had continued to live in the house next door to his mother-in-law. (The father-in-law was dead.) He had married for the third time so that his children would be taken care of. Now his wife was in charge of all his affairs, he being retired and developing a reputation as a wise and successful mystical curer *(ḍukun)*. He had discovered that his wife was spending his children's money too fast and sending home large sums to her own family. Pak Subroto was a quiet, mild man, and he said nothing, perhaps knowing that sooner or later the mother of his second wife who lived next door would handle the problem—which she did by a campaign of constant quarreling with the wife, not speaking to her for weeks on end, and generally making life miserable for her, until finally the wife asked Pak Subroto for a divorce. He seemed to consider it beneath his dignity as a mystic and aristocrat to engage in divorce proceedings, and forced his wife to go to the various religious officials by herself to get the divorce. Soon after this, he married again, this time a woman who could save money and who was able to get along with his mother-in-law.

This case illustrates not only the need for agreement on economic matters to keep a marriage stable but also some other characteristics of Javanese family life. It demonstrates the Javanese husband's tendency to withdraw from the affairs of his household, leaving them almost entirely in the hands of women. It suggests that it is crucially important that the women get along together and that the antagonisms between men or those between men and women are not so disruptive as those between women. It also bears out what has been said about the various tensions between affinal relatives: that each one's primary loyalty lies with the consanguineal kin, and that this conflict can further divide a marriage.

A third reason for divorce sometimes mentioned by Javanese is conflict between affinal relatives. Although such a conflict may underlie many divorces, it is rarely given as a precipitating cause.

Usually tensions with relatives outside the immediate nuclear family are alleviated by moving away rather than by divorce. However, I encountered an example of divorce which showed how dependent a young Javanese couple are on their parents. A boy and girl were engaged in childhood by their parents, small urban tradesmen, who were neighbors. Eventually they married and had a child. Soon after the birth of the child the two pairs of parents had a quarrel and, completely against the desires of the married couple, who were content together, insisted on their divorce.

The fourth explanation commonly given at the time of divorce is that the couple just do not like each other and so will not sleep or live with each other. That this is the reason given in perhaps the majority of the cases is hardly strange in view of the custom of marrying with little or no previous contact, which necessitates selection or rejection *after* the wedding. Young couples who have their marriages arranged without their participation are likely to divorce for apparently minor reasons.

Successful Javanese marriages are not easy to explain either in general or in the particular case. Javanese merely say, if a couple have been married a long time with no trouble, that they "fit" (*djodo* or *tjotjog*), a term with metaphysical implications which is also used, for instance, to refer to the mysterious relationship between a patient and the particular curer who has finally made him well. If the marriage fails they did not "fit." Happiness in marriage is thought to be dependent on several factors, the most important of which is the relationship between the respective dates of birth of the couple, partly because these determine the character (*tabiat*) of the individual and hence which partner he or she can get along best with. Another computation that is extremely important is the setting of the day and time of the wedding; and one of the magical measures that can be taken to prevent the break-up of a marriage is to perform the wedding again on a more magically auspicious occasion. Juminah, who had frequent quarrels with her husband, was told by a wise man (*guru*) that their trouble was that they had been married on the wrong day. When he had figured out a better day for them, they gave a special ritual meal just like that at a wedding, but simpler and with only one witness and the religious officer. Evidently, this ritual reaffirmation of the marriage (called *bangun nikah*, "to build up the marriage") provided considerable support to Juminah and Karto's shaky marriage. Javanese consider it important to have such a ritual meal also after a serious quarrel in which the husband has said, "I divorce you!" but has not gone through with it, because the very saying of the words has power, and unless steps are taken they will be divorced, in fact, by the death of one of them.

Djodo means more than simply that the two people will like each other's company; it also indicates that they will prosper. Many stories were told to me to prove this—stories in which husband and wife with previous spouses were poor, and who, when they married again, suddenly became rich. (Soon, however, in these stories, one of the two is unfaithful and the other gets sick worrying about it, or they get a divorce; and, in the end, they both become extremely poor again.)

The concept of *djodo* is a rationalizing concept rather than a motivating idea: it neither makes people try harder nor allows them to try less hard to make the marriage a success. People do not usually marry until they have been assured by the numbers that they will *djodo;* and if they do not *djodo*, some explanation —an error of computation or an overlooked factor—can always be found.

The main reason Javanese give as a motive for trying to stay married in the face of disruptive pressures is concern for the children. The mother, in particular, feels this concern because she knows that, if she were unable to support all of her children herself after divorce, some of them might have to go to live with their father and a stepmother, which is not a pleasant prospect, since Javanese strongly differentiate their own children from others and treat them with favoritism. The mother has no such urgency to maintain a marriage if she can take the children with her, since it is not thought that a child *must* have a father or that a stepfather is bad.

In conclusion, the inference to be drawn from the several

concrete situations commonly leading to divorce which are illustrated in the foregoing discussion is that the frequency of divorce in Java is best explained as the result of the general sociological conditions surrounding Javanese marriage.

On the one side of the ledger, factors opposing divorce are few. Javanese women, especially, but perhaps also men, are concerned about the welfare of their children, and it is believed that the child's own parents love him most. To a man concerned about his economic welfare a woman is almost indispensable, not only to keep his household going but also often on the productive side of affairs; and a wife, because she shares equally the profits and losses, is a more valuable partner than other women who might have conflicting loyalties. There may be some concern for insuring that one has a partner for one's old age, but this would be a minor concern because an old parent can depend on the support of his grown children whether or not both parents are together.

On the other side, the factors facilitating, if not encouraging, divorce are several. There are no institutionalized aspects of the Javanese kinship system, such as bride-price or unfavorable settlement of property after divorce, to discourage a couple from ending their marriage. A divorce does not disrupt social arrangements for an entire kin group; it makes no difference to other members of the kindred whether a marriage continues or not. The kinship system not only does not inhibit divorce; it works to facilitate divorce since children of a divorced couple are always easily added to the families of their siblings and the divorced girl always has a place in her parents' family. Marriage by arrangement, together with the absence of strong means for enforcing the marriage, results in the exercise of personal choice *after* the marriage; and, even in the absence of arrangement, the custom of making personal choices on snap judgments and without a courting period comes to the same result. The universally accepted participation of women in the productive side of the Javanese economic system, and the range of fully supporting occupations a woman can enter, offer a Javanese woman ample opportunity to be independent of a husband's support.

Old Age

When Javanese become old and no longer are heads of complete households, no longer have young children, and no longer can produce enough to live on, their children or their sibling's children or their grandchildren take them into their homes. In general, old people are considered to be entitled to great respect, and many live out their years justly receiving such respect because of their superior knowledge of mystical and practical matters. But for those who become helpless or senile, the respect for the aged may be scant and grudgingly given. I have seen a child-like old woman teased in a way that no fully functioning Javanese would permit; and I have seen such an old woman being ordered to be quiet in a manner usually reserved for disobedient six-year-olds. However, neither of these old women was the real parent of the head of the household; one was a grandmother, the other was the sister of a grandmother. Her son or daughter would probably have been more reserved and respectful.

One middle-aged *prijaji*, Pak Wiro, who had taken care of both his old parents until their death, said that, at least for *prijajis*, it is not nice to say that the old person "lives with" the young person because this draws attention to his dependency; one should say, rather that the young person "lives with" the older person, or "is being taken care of" by the old person. He explained that if it were said that the old man "lived with" the young people it would imply that he was their servant, which would be insulting.

By the time a person is old and single again, he has moved out of the center of a going nuclear family and becomes one of the "outsiders" who join the household. He is likely to be in a semi-dependent role (having often transferred most of his property already into the hands of his children), and must fit himself into a household which includes at least one person (for instance, a son-in-law) who is not a blood relative. This situation can be uncomfortable at times, but usually an old person's life is fairly serene. He or she is useful in caring for the children of the household, and there is usually a warm, informal relationship between the oldster and the youngsters of the house who are, like him, also in a sense peripheral to the adult world.

6. JAVANESE VALUES AND THE JAVANESE FAMILY

The family, in any society, is the bridge between the individual and his culture. The intimate family group and the more extended network of kinsmen provide each person with basic models for social relationships with the rest of the world. His childhood experiences in particular are given fundamental form by the institutional structures of the family, and it is through these experiences that he gains the understanding, emotional equipment and, above all, the moral commitments which make it possible for him, as an adult, to act as a full-fledged member of his society.

Certain diffuse, general social values provide legitimacy and meaning to familial institutions and serve as normative guides for the daily give-and-take among family members. These same social values may also be important elements in some non-familial institutions, such as the structure of authority and social control within the community. It is very likely, too, that these moral components of familial institutions are internalized by the child during his earliest and most impressionable years, and become significant motivating forces within his personality.

Two distinctively Javanese values have appeared often in the foregoing description of Javanese family life. While the two together are not the only moral guides underlying Javanese kinship behavior, they are of central importance to it. These are, first, the cluster of values involved in the Javanese view of the etiquette of "respect," and secondly, those concerned with the Javanese emphasis on the maintenance of "harmonious social appearances." They are closely related, and together represent important forces for the cohesion and resiliency of the Javanese family and, also, of Javanese society as it is today.

However, the mere presence of any particular value in a cultural tradition does not, in itself, ensure its active pursuit nor its attainment. At times it may conflict with other, equally desirable values. Shifts in the social structure such as a change in the sources of power may make it irrelevant. Situational factors such as poverty may inhibit action in terms of the value. Or it may be psychologically difficult for the members of the society to act in terms of it. The two values discussed here are no exception to these realistic limiting factors; however, the Javanese are fairly successful much of the time in their attempts to behave according to them, both within their families and their communities. One measure of their success are certain "costs" or undesirable indirect consequences of modeling their behavior in the direction of their ideals.

The first of these values, the proper expression of "respect" (what the Javanese refer to as showing *urmat* or feeling *sungkan*) is based on the traditional Javanese view that all social relationships are hierarchically ordered, and on the moral imperative to maintain and express this mode of social order as a good in itself. The second one (summed up in Javanese as *rukun*), the determination to "maintain harmonious social appearances," to minimize the overt expression of any kind of social and personal conflict, is based on the Javanese view that emotional equilibrium, emotional stasis, is of highest worth, and on the corresponding moral imperative to control one's own impulses, to keep them out of awareness or at least unexpressed, so as not to set up reverberating emotional responses in others.

The cluster of attitudes centering on "respect" is a guide to social behavior in many different contexts—toward government officials, in the schools, in the political parties, in relationships among neighbors, among others. Although in modern Java the bases for social prestige are changing, and it is also increasingly easier for an individual to move upwards in general status during his lifetime, the traditional view persists that all men are socially unequal, and the customary etiquette patterns are still followed for all relationships of any sort between inferior and superior. The diffuse claims for protection, gifts and help in trouble that an inferior can make on his superior, and their reverse, the diffuse respect and loyalty that a superior can ask from an inferior, serve to bind together people who may, in a complexly changing society, have sharply opposed interests. Preservation of the forms of etiquette thus operates to stabilize and solidify social relationships of every sort, and serves as a strongly integrative force in Javanese society.

We have seen how relationships within the extended kinship group and also within the nuclear family have hierarchical elements, and we have traced how the child learns the attitudes appropriate to these status differences. The kinship terminology itself provides a framework of status distinctions among kinsmen, each term representing a position slightly higher or lower than the next, status distinctions which are recognized in everyday social usage. The child's earliest interaction with his kinsmen requires the learning and practice of the customs of deferential behavior. Within the nuclear family too, the same ranking system is found again, in miniature. The relationship of the father to the rest of the family, and those of older siblings to younger ones, are also strongly characterized by the observance of patterns of polite respect on the one hand and restrained aloofness on the other.

"Respect" in this Javanese sense means only the recognition of superior rank by means of the appropriate forms of etiquette. No authority, power, nor any important privileges follow directly from higher rank as such. Nevertheless, the Javanese place great emotional weight on the proper observance of the proprieties of deference in all phases of social intercourse. This emotional emphasis derives mainly from the role that the whole respect cluster plays in the socialization of the Javanese child. The early age at which training in this area is initiated, and the effect the pattern has on his parents' behavior toward him, means that the values associated with status and respect must be deeply internalized forces within Javanese personalities.

The same can be said of the second cluster of attitudes, those concerned with the maintenance of the appearance if not the substance of "social harmony," for the sake of inner psychic equilibrium. These too are inculcated in the child and affect his familial relationships at ages and in ways which must exert an important influence on the development of his personality. The term *rukun* is often on his parents' lips. It signifies a state of agreement, of unanimity in a group concerning its means and purposes, at least in outer behavior. If there is no overt expression of divisive opinions and feelings, then the group is said to be in *rukun*. Thus, in practice *rukun* actually refers not to mutual aid and co-operation but to the *appearance* of such and to the absence of overt interpersonal conflict. This state is considered to be highly desirable though not always attainable in any situation where decisions are to be made and actions carried out by more than one person. It is commonly invoked in those situations involving division or distribution of material goods, as a counterweight to individual greed and to the harboring and expression of resentment and disappointment after the decision has been made.

The conception of *rukun* as an active element in all aspects of Javanese social organization—whether the valued state is actually striven for, for instance in traditional village meetings, or mourned for its absence, as in situations of economic and political conflict, or whether the value is invoked as a traditional sanction for modern innovations, as President Sukarno did when he presented his proposals in 1956 for a "National Council" which would make governmental decisions by unanimous agreement rather than through the dissension of political parties speaking through their parliamentary representatives.

Within the sphere of kinship the *rukun* value is a central element. It is held up as an ideal for all relationships, from those between siblings to those between distant cousins. For instance, in the settlement of inheritance cases, the desire to achieve a harmonious solution in which no intense feelings of resentment remain, or at least are not expressed, kinsmen look for compromise solutions, setting aside if need be the traditional inheritance rules in favor of a substantive equity which takes into account the real needs of all concerned. The fact that the customary rules are not always legalistically adhered to in such cases of inheritance, divorce settlement and adoption is, however, by no means a sign of the "detraditionalization" or "individualization" of Javanese society; rather it is an evidence of the continued countering influence of the equally traditional procedural norm for *rukun*.

Striving after *rukun* is often the main motivation for helping a relative in time of trouble in spite of mutual distrust and personal selfishness. Sharing one's home and possessions is difficult under the extreme conditions of poverty of most Javanese, but the moral pressure to avoid disappointing a kinsman and to minimize conflict within the family is strong. Nevertheless, relatives are often neglected and families do break up. In fact, the Javanese are successful in achieving *rukun* in governing their communities and families only part of the time.

During the Javanese child's first years, even before he can comprehend in any coherent way such concepts as "respect" and "the maintenance of social harmony," the psychological preparations are made. Both of these values require the ability to sharply inhibit one's behavior, to choose inaction rather than action. The general treatment of the infant, from his gentle swaddling to the full support of the shawl at his mother's hip and the constant protection from any unpleasant shock, is all in the direction of encouraging a deeply passive attitude. While inhibition and passivity are by no means identical, a passive approach to the world makes inhibition considerably easier. This passivity is further reinforced throughout childhood by the mother's vigilant supervision which stifles any exercise of initiative before its inception. The first learning of polite behavior is passive: the repetitive pushing away of the baby's left hand and pulling out of his right hand to force him to perform the proper gesture for giving and taking. And, the later learning of the forms of etiquette is also passive, as the adults tirelessly reiterate the polite words and phrases that the child should be saying, until he imitates them correctly.

Hypersensitivity to subtle reactions of other people is a personality characteristic also needed for the adequate observance of "respect" and maintenance of "social harmony." The mother's discouraging any spontaneous behavior by her diligent watchfulness and constant instruction probably fosters a sensitivity to her responses, a sensitivity which is further sharpened later by the father's gradual concealment of his own feelings toward the child, and substitution of a formal dignified demeanor.

Two events occur after the child's first year which although they may not be traumatic, are probably deeply disturbing: weaning and learning to walk. The weaning experience is notable for the inconsistent attitude of the mother who feels unsure about making this first real denial to the child and who sometimes alternately prohibits and permits the child to nurse, giving in when the child protests loudly enough. She continues this same inconsistency in giving and refusing other food throughout the child's first years. The consequence of this indecisiveness on the part of the mother may be a deep conviction that if one cries long enough one will get what one wants, and an inability to accept frustration as final, an attitude which if it persists in adults must require strong moral pressure, such as that represented in the ideal of *rukun,* to counteract it. The second event, learning to walk, coming as it does with no preliminary crawling period, may be an experience which places great strain on the sense of equilibrium. At any rate, most Javanese have an exquisite sense of balance and fine bodily grace. The concern for physical balance is congruent with the deep cultural emphasis on psychic equilibrium.

To a certain extent the permissive indulgence of infancy continues into early childhood and the child has a warm, though intermittent, relationship with his father in this period. However, increasingly, pressure is put on him to behave in a mannerly, quiet and docile way. As younger siblings come along he is forced to repress his own desires and to defer to their wishes, giving him his first lessons in the inhibition of any expression of a response to frustration. The primary sanction applied to the child to achieve these goals of obedience and self-control is the mother's threat that some agency outside the family—evil spirits, dogs or strangers will hurt him if he does not behave. The fear of the outsider becomes closely associated with the pressure for proper behavior.

In later childhood, "proper behavior" no longer has to be enforced by direct threats of being hurt, but more indirect hints of disapproval are sufficient. The child is now taught not to be frightened of strangers but to worry about their opinion of him. Consistently, it is not the mother's own disapproval, nor, at first, the father's, that is held over the disobedient child, but that of non-family members, "other people." He is taught to feel "isin" toward these outsiders, to dread the feeling of embarrassment, shame, and guilt that he learns to associate with the open expression of feeling or the transgression of other rules of etiquette.

The critical event at this point is the shift in the role of the father, from being a warm, accepting companion to a distant, dignified stranger, whom the mother equates in her admonitions with the outsiders toward whom one formerly felt fear, and with whom one is now carefully circumspect. This, presumably has two general psychological effects on the child: first there must be considerable disappointment and a feeling that his father is now rejecting him, and second, the outside world with all its concern over status differences and etiquette has now entered the intimacy of the family, bringing with it all its constraint and formality. Javanese culture, in contrast to that for instance of Japan which has a similar stress on interpersonal formality, provides no area of life where the rules of propriety are held in abeyance and the person can relax.

The Javanese child is drawn into this system of rigid self-control and deference in interpersonal relationships as early as the age of five, and he learns well the lesson that it is morally right, aesthetically pleasing, and psychologically rewarding to observe the appropriate etiquette of respect toward all superiors, above all, toward his father. The emotional side of respectful behavior is not merely *isin*, anxiety over not conforming, but *sungkan*, the feeling of embarrassed shrinking into the self, the graceful constraint of one's own personality out of deference to the other person. To "know" *isin*, *sungkan*, and *rukun* and to know when and how they are appropriate is to have attained the more general ideal of being *djawa*: being proper, sane, and mature, in short being fully Javanese.

These ideals, then, play a significant part in setting the emotional tone or ethos of familial relations in Java. To the extent that they are achieved in actual day-to-day life, however, they entail certain "costs." That is, some of the perhaps undesirable features of Javanese life can be seen as indirect results of their adhering to the norms for etiquette and external social harmony. Both of these norms entail the concealment of all dissonant wishes or feelings. Commitment to them makes it completely distasteful to a Javanese to oppose directly the will of another person, or to express hostility openly. The only practical alternative in such situations is evasion, covert disobedience, and mutual avoidance. The prevalence and length of quarrels by avoidance *(satru)* between kinsmen, spouses, and even parents and children is a result. To some extent too, the frequency of divorce can be traced to this same normative source. And lastly, the careful and cold distance that is maintained between the nuclear family and its secondary and affinal relatives is to a large degree the consequence of the commitment to a value for the appearance rather than the substance of mutual aid.

The structure of the Javanese family, in terms of behavioral expectations placed on even the youngest members, thus schools them in the fundamental rules and attitudes necessary for proper adult relationships with his neighbors, superiors and inferiors. Within the household, the role he must play vis-a-vis his father and older brothers gives him the essential forms for the expression of differential status, while the diversely ranked roles he must play toward his other kinsmen give him an opportunity to practise the variations. Similarly he learns in interaction with his siblings and later with his more distant relatives the valued attitudes associated with the coordination of group action, particularly important in village and neighborhood organization.

This, then, is the major contribution that the family and kinship system make to the functioning of Javanese society: the cultivation and preservation in the individual, through his experience in his family, of primary ethical norms, norms which enable each Javanese to pursue a way of life which is morally acceptable, personally satisfying, and at the same time which integrates and sustains the fabric of the whole society.

JAVANESE KINSHIP TERMINOLOGY

I. TERMS OF REFERENCE FOR CONSANGUINEAL KIN

mbah
(ejang*) grandparent, grandparent's sibling, grandparent's cousin, i.e., any relative on the same generation level as grandparent, and any spouse of these.

bapak
(pak, rama) father, or any male member of parent's generation, or spouse of a woman called ibu.

ibu
(bu, mbok, simbok, bijung, mak) mother, or any female member of parent's generation, or spouse of man called bapak.

pak ḍé
(derived from bapak geḍé, literally, "big father") parent's brother older than parent, son of grandparent's sibling older than grandparent, or spouse of a woman called bu ḍé. (Ego calls pak ḍé any man whom ego's parent calls mas.)

bu ḍé
(mbok ḍé) parent's sister older than parent, daughter of grandparent's sibling older than grandparents, or spouse of man called pak ḍé. (Ego calls bu ḍé any woman whom ego's parent calls mbakju.)

pak lik
(derived from bapak tjilik, literally, "little father"; paman, man, lik) parent's brother younger than parent, son of grandparent's sibling younger than grandparent, or spouse of woman called bu lik. (Ego calls pak lik any man whom ego's parent calls ḍik.)

---

*Alternate forms, usage determined by class and geographic location.

bu lik	*(bik, mbok lik)* parent's sister younger than parent, daughter of grandparent's sibling younger than grandparent, or spouse of man called *pak lik*. (Ego calls *bu lik* any woman whom ego's parent calls *dik*.)
mas	*(kangmas, kang, gus)* older brother, son of parent's older sibling, son of grandparent's older sibling's child, or spouse of any woman ego calls *mbakju*.
mbakju	*(mbak, ju)* older sister, daughter of parent's older sibling, daughter of grandparent's older sibling's child, or spouse of any man whom ego calls *mas*.
adik	*(dik, raji, djeng)* younger sibling, child of parent's younger sibling, child of grandparent's younger sibling's child, or spouse of person whom ego calls *dik*.
mas misanan	(from *pisan*, "once") son of parent's older sibling.
mbakju misanan	daughter of parent's older sibling.
adik misanan	child of parent's younger sibling.
mas mindoan	(from *pindo*, "twice") son of grandparent's older sibling's child.
mbakju mindoan	daughter of grandparent's older sibling's child.
adik mindoan	child of grandparent's younger sibling's child.
anak	*(nak, joga, putra)* child.
keponakan	(derived from *anak*, "child"; *kepénakan*) child of ego's sibling, child of ego's cousin.
putu	*(wajah)* grandchild.
putu ponakan	grandchild of ego's sibling, grandchild of ego's cousin.
bujut	great-grandchild, great-grandchild of ego's sibling, great-grandchild of ego's cousin; great-grandparent, sibling or cousin of great-grandparent.

tjanggah*   great-grandchild's child, or anyone of the same generation; great-grandparent's parent, or anyone of the same generation.

warèng*   great-grandchild's grandchild, or anyone of the same generation; great-grandparent's grandparent, or anyone of the same generation.

uḍeg-uḍeg*   great-grandchild's great-grandchild, or anyone of the same generation; great-grandparent's great-grandparent, or anyone of the same generation.

gantung siwur*   great-grandchild's great-grandchild's child, or anyone of the same generation; great-grandparent's great-grandparent's parent, or anyone of the same generation.

II. TERMS OF ADDRESS FOR CONSANGUINEAL KIN

mbah   is addressed as *mbah* or *éjang*.

bapak   *pak, rama*. (Occasionally *bapak* is used, but in these cases it has the connotation of respectful third person.)

ibu   *bu, mbok, simbok, bijung, mak*. (Occasionally *ibu* is used, but in these cases it has the connotation of respectful third person.)

pak ḍé   *pak ḍé.*

bu ḍe   *bu ḍe, mbok ḍé.*

pak lik   *pak lik, paman, man, lik.*

bu lik   *bu lik, bik, mbok lik.*

mas   *mas, kangmas, kang, gus.*

mbakju   *mbakju, mbak, ju.*

*These terms are rarely used and appear to be merely a logical elaboration of the generational aspect of the kinship system.

adik   *ḍik*, or familiar terms such as *lé* (boy) or *nḍuk* (girl), or by the name alone.

mas misanan }
mas minḍoan }   *mas, kang, kangmas, gus.*

mbakju misanan }
mbakju minḍoan }   *mbakju, mbak, ju.*

aḍik misanan }
aḍik minḍoan }   *ḍik*, or other familiar terms.

anak
keponakan   }   *nak*, or, more frequently, by name or by fa-
putu   }   miliar terms such as *lé, nduk*.
putu ponakan   }

bujut   if great-grandchild, is addressed as *nak*, or, more frequently, by name, or by familiar terms such as *lé, nduk;* if great-grandparent, as *mbah* or *mbah bujut.*

III. TERMS OF REFERENCE AND ADDRESS FOR AFFINAL RELATIVES

bodjo   *(rajat, sémah)* spouse.

sing wédok   *(ingkang èstri, aḍiné, ibuné, mbokné, rajiné, kantja èstri)* wife; addressed as "little sister" *(ḍik, djeng)* or teknonymously *(mbokné S——, ibuné S——).*

sing lanang   *(ingkang djaler, masé, bapaké, kantja djaler)* husband; addressed as "older brother" *(mas, kangmas, kang)* or teknonymously *(bapaké S——, paké S——, mbahé S——).*

maratuwa   *(marasepuh)* spouse's parent; addressed as "mother" *(bu,* etc.) or as "father" *(pak,* etc.).

anak mantu   child's spouse; addressed as "child" *(nak)* or by name, familiar term, or teknonymously.

mas ipé	older sibling's husband or spouse's older brother; addressed as "older brother" (*mas*, etc.).
mbakju ipé	older sibling's wife or spouse's older sister; addressed as "older sister" (*mbakju*, etc.).
aḍik ipé	younger sibling's spouse or spouse's younger sibling; addressed as "younger sibling" (*ḍik*, etc.).
bésan	parent of child's spouse; addressed in formal polite manner.

Spouses of relatives other than those mentioned above are referred to descriptively as "spouse of So-and-so" (*bodjoné S——*), and addressed as if they were kin, thus: the wife of *pak ḍé* is *bu ḍé*. Kin of spouse, with the exception of those mentioned above, are also referred to descriptively and addressed following spouse's usage.

Javanese Kinship Terms of Reference

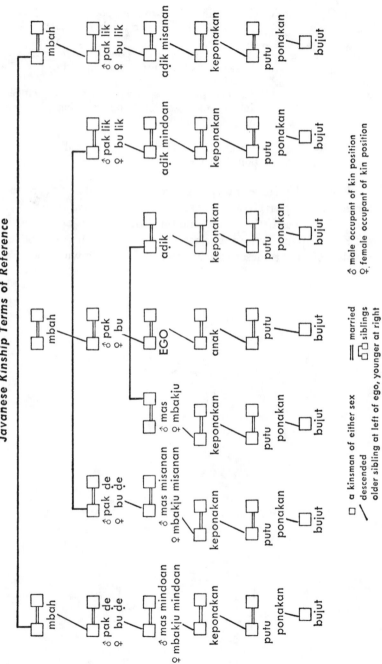

♂ male occupant of kin position
♀ female occupant of kin position

━━━ married
◻◻ siblings

◻ a kinsman of either sex

descended

older sibling at left of ego, younger at right

METHODS OF RESEARCH

SINCE this study was one of the first in Java to utilize modern field research methods and recent anthropological orientations, it was necessary to make a rather thorough ethnographic coverage of all aspects of Javanese life and to avoid too great a specialization of interest which would interfere with the gathering of this basic data. The presence in the field of a number of other researchers made it possible to divide the labor somewhat, but each of us had to make our own "map" of Javanese culture. As a result, a good deal of my research—into the Javanese dance, modern Indonesian novels, household and commercial costs, the growing and processing of rice and other crops, labor union organization, schools and teaching methods, medical practices and beliefs, to name a few—is not apparent in the present report. But the results of it are there: an anthropologist is never quite sure which aspect of his work will be most fruitful; and sometimes in the course of investigation of a most unlikely segment of a culture, a clue will appear that illuminates all the previous material collected with a specific theoretic aim in view.

The material presented in this study was obtained primarily from interviews of representative citizens of Modjokuto and from observation of their behavior with their families and neighbors during a fifteen-month period.

In discussing techniques of gathering data, there are two major questions to be answered: 1) how was the object for study isolated and selected, and 2) what was the instrument used for extracting and recording data about this object? Since the anthropological object ultimately is some group of interacting human beings and the instrument is the anthropologist himself as he interacts with these people, the division of the problem in practice is artificial, and the question becomes as one of defining and describing the social context of the research itself. What was the preparation and orientation of the anthropologist? How was, first, the community and, second, the component social group or individuals chosen for study? How representative were this community and these social groups and individuals of this particular statistical universe? What were the roles engaged in by the anthropologist vis-à-vis these groups and individuals? What were the means available to him for verifying the validity and reliability of his insights? The following paragraphs are an attempt to give partial answers to some of these questions.

The first step in preparation for the field trip was becoming familiar with the literature on Java, which meant learning to read Dutch. After some work at Harvard, my husband and I spent three months in Holland, working at the Tropical Institute in Amsterdam and the University Library at Leiden. At that time I worked particularly on the extensive literature on *adat*, or customary, law. We left Holland for Indonesia in October, 1952.

More important than the knowledge of the past literature for a field worker with general interests is knowledge of the native language. We were fortunate to have, before we left, an intensive one-year course at Harvard in spoken Indonesian. Although we knew that Indonesian would not be spoken in a small town, it is closely related to Javanese in its phonemic system and basic morphology. When we arrived in Djokjakarta, one of the two court cities in Central Java, we immediately began study of Javanese with informants. After five months of full-time language work, we were able to dispense with interpreters, and when we entered the town of Modjokuto, in May, 1953, to begin research, we could make our way alone. This was extremely important, for it set our role immediately as one radically different from that of all other newly arrived foreigners in Java, and it was the first major step toward our being accepted.

Since my husband and I were part of a team of field workers, this fact had significant effects on our roles. There were adjustments to be made in relating to one another that had repercussions on the way we were seen by the rest of the people in Modjokuto. Since we had all known each other and worked together for more than a year, we had realistic expectations about the kind of co-operation which would be most productive. We decided, even before entering Modjokuto, to divide the task at hand into several rough fields: the Chinese community, the village life, social organization of the town, the town market, religion and family life. We worked, by and large, separately, had few meetings, and conferred with each other only occasionally on topics of mutual interest. This meant that each of us was free to go at the task of relating to the Javanese around him in his own way. Most of the people of Modjokuto knew us only as individuals, even though they were aware that we were a group. We were not often seen together, and we tried to avoid using the same informants.

We chose from the beginning to make no attempts to hide or "reinterpret" our roles as anthropologists; it would have been next to impossible, with the size of our group and the sophistication of the Javanese, for us to maintain any false roles during the entire period we were there. We told anyone who asked exactly what we were doing, the explanation being limited only by the comprehension of the questioner. I believe that this directness was respected by the Javanese, although several very good informants were nevertheless worried throughout our stay by the suspicion that we might be spies for the American government. We presented ourselves as we were—a group of students from Harvard University who wanted to study the "life and culture" of the Javanese. This explanation was fully comprehensible to them for several reasons: the student role is a common one in Java; the idea of going to a foreign country for "experience" and curiosity is a common wish; and the Javanese often look upon their own culture with a sort of ethnological objectivity.

The fact that we were a team with varied interests affected the choice of town. We needed a town which was not too unusual (if that was possible; no two Javanese towns are alike), one which included a well developed market, a good representation of various governmental levels, a fair-sized Chinese population, a variety of types of villages surrounding it, and a normal balance of religious and political groups. After a number of tours through Central and East Java, we settled on Modjokuto, which met our criteria and had a number of practical advantages: security, adequate housing possibilities, and an intelligent and sympathetic District Head in charge.

Once the actual field study had begun, the problem before us was a difficult one: how to adapt traditional anthropological field methods to such a complex society? Was it possible to pick a small group of interacting people to study intensively, to isolate a primary group that would be representative of the larger society? Actually, it was not. The whole town had to be our subject of study; one neighborhood alone would not be sufficient. And even though my husband and I chose to concentrate mainly on the town, since one member of the field team and his wife were working on village life, our contacts with townsmen constantly led us out into the countryside to village relatives, political or commercial associates, and others. We found, as the study progressed, that each social structural segment had a different geographic referent: while a few of the poorest members of the town oriented themselves around a particular neighborhood and rarely went away from town, traders and civil servants saw themselves as members of a region-wide interacting social group, traveling to and from various towns and cities and contracting their marriages as much outside the Modjokuto area as within it.

The task was one of grasping fairly quickly the major axes of social differentiation, and making sure that no important social segment was left unrepresented by a good informant. It was a matter of weighting and emphasis: how much intensive knowledge of individuals should be sacrificed to the need for wide representation, and how much extensive coverage should be sacrificed to the need for that deeper understanding of the culture that only comes after long conversations with a willing informant. This was a dilemma which was never finally solved, which entered into each decision in every day's work. It was clear from the beginning that this meant that my role had to be in certain aspects one of the stranger; that my initial lack of ties to any particular social group had to be maintained; that I could not afford to be identified with those of high education or those of wealth or, on the other hand, with a single neighborhood of lower class women. My mobility was essential to the success of the study. I was unsure what effect this would have on my relationships with the women of Modjokuto, but it gradually became evident that a Javanese woman's role is by no means limited to kitchen and cradle. Since there are energetic professional woman traders who travel freely over the countryside, and there are woman teachers and nurses, although the Javanese had never seen a woman anthropologist, a woman with a job to do was quite comprehensible.

My husband and I moved to Modjokuto in May, 1953, the vanguard of the field team. We moved first into a large brick and concrete house that served as our group's field headquarters and began making formal visits to all the members of the elite in town: the top government officials, the heads of political parties, the richer merchants, the older teachers. My husband and I went together on these visits and divided the task of recording between us. We took no notes during these interviews, with the occasional exception of jotting down a difficult Javanese word, a proper name, or, at the second or third visit, some unemotionally toned ethnographic information, such as the names of the months, the religious holidays, the types of schools. Each day, usually in the afternoon when most of Modjokuto napped, we typed full accounts of our experiences, repeating the conversations as nearly verbatim as our memories allowed. This first month was one of polite feeling of our way; we tried to meet every person with prestige and power and to avoid topics that were potentially disturbing to rapport either for ourselves or for the rest of our group. After a week three members of the field team arrived, followed a week later by two more, and, after several more weeks, by the last. The gradualness of entry was partly the result of a policy of minimizing any appearance of solidarity so that the people of Modjokuto could meet us as individuals rather than en masse. At the end of the month, my husband suddenly came down with pneumonia, and he and I were forced to return to Djokjakarta, where he spent two months in a hospital.

When we returned we moved directly into the house of Pak

Ardjo. This house had been located for us by the District Head, and we had already established a good relationship with Pak Ardjo during our first month in Modjokuto. During the period of our absence, the house had been occupied by Mr. and Mrs. Jay. The house was on one of the main roads of the town; it had a cement floor and waist-high cement walls, and the upper parts of the wall were of whitewashed woven bamboo. There was electricity (enough power for one 25 watt lamp), and the windows were only wooden shutters. The family living in it was that of a railroad machinist, his wife, his youngest son, aged ten, and his adult daughter who had been married and divorced three times and now lived at home with a twelve-year-old daughter and a five-year-old son. They said they would rent the main four rooms of the house to us and move into two smaller rooms at the side which had a separate entrance, and that we could share their daily food. My husband and I chose to live in it because it was one of an ordinary townsman, and because we wanted to live with a family rather than by ourselves. The intimacy and close quarters were difficult to bear at times, but the profits were greater than we expected. Pak and Bu Ardjo were among our best informants in many areas of Javanese life; and our participation in their everyday affairs and family crises gave us insights that no amount of direct, formal interviewing could have elicited. We lived with the Ardjo's continuously until October, 1954 when we returned to the United States.

My husband's sickness and subsequent convalescence gave us a chance to break off strong ties with the elite segment of the town population, with the exception of those individuals we had selected as potential informants. For the first few months after our return I worked mainly on building relationships with the Ardjo family and with our neighbors, and my husband was developing a wider range of contacts in the town.

At first I spent most of my time with Pak Ardjo's wife, Bu Ardjo, a woman of about sixty who was already a great-grandmother. I watched her cooking, went to market with her, went calling on her relatives, joined a neighborhood woman's credit union club, and went to funerals, weddings, and circumcisions with her. She treated me very much as her own daughter, taught me, scolded me for my stupidity, and advised me about my social behavior. The three children in the household gradually became accustomed to us and took occasional trips with us. It was against the detailed background of this best-known family with whom we lived more than a year that I began to build up a more abstract picture of general patterns of the family life of Javanese townsmen.

However, I began to find out that my strong position within the Ardjo family had its drawbacks. I began to become acquainted with the people of the neighborhood and, simultaneously, to discover the limits of the Ardjo's social circle. I found out that some neighbors would have little to do with me because of my ties to the Ardjo's, and that certainly none of them, whether friends of the Ardjo's or not, would tell me anything concrete about their feelings toward people either within their families or outside them for fear that derogatory gossip would get back to Bu Ardjo.

The Ardjo's were not of the town elite. Pak Ardjo was respected among his neighbors for his age (and, secretly, for his magical powers) and for the fact that he held a job as railroad repairman which brought in a regular monthly check. The Ardjo's were embarrassed but pleased when someone from the elite group came calling on us—and embarrassed and annoyed when we brought in people from class-positions lower than they. We found that lower status neighbors would resist relationships with us because of this feeling. A further social distinction soon became apparent: that of ideological commitment to one of several opposing traditions, most particularly the general split between those people who took their Islam seriously and those who prefer the more indigenous, animistic variant of the Javanese religion. The Ardjo's fell definitely in the second category, and when, as my husband's work brought him in contact with pious Moslems, a group of shawled Moslem women came calling on me, Bu Ardjo's displeasure was plainly evident.

This, then, was the problem: how to establish close relationships with people who were of different social segments from those with whom we were living; how to disengage ourselves from the Ardjo's enough to enable forming new ties, but not so much as to lose their valuable support and the fruitful entree into their family. It was at this point that we began to define our roles more clearly as that of researcher. We began to expand our social activities to include people from other neighborhoods, and we explained to the Ardjo's that it was important for our work that we know people from all ways of life. One of the difficulties of interviewing Javanese in their own homes is that they are rarely alone and that, when in a group of more than two, they are more comfortable in a formal, contentless conversation. We tried to bring our informants to our own home, but we ran into difficulties with the Ardjos' definition of these calls; since it was their house, they often felt, as hosts, that they should join in the conversations. We devised a scheme which would tactfully emphasize that this was work, not social calling, and would simultaneously move our callers out of earshot; we had a wooden partition put in one of our rooms and labeled the new room an "office." Here we were able to work quietly and steadily alone with informants. (Here, too, I was later able to set up a dictaphone and give 35 T.A.T.'s. The results of these tests, however, have not been used for the present report.)

During the entire field work period we were constantly meeting new people and filling in details on the general population of the area. My husband and I interviewed the various governmental heads, collected statistics and reports from them, spoke to members of different occupations about their work, and met the heads of private organizations such as political parties, buying co-operatives, charitable organizations, and dance and orchestral groups. All these relationships were simple, direct, and short-lived.

For the purposes of the present study, however, I needed to find people with whom I could have something close to a friendship relationship, persons who would take me into their homes naturally and who would talk to me at length about themselves and their families. The Ardjo family was a very good start. I had met, in the very first month, an intelligent, leftist woman schoolteacher with three children, and I soon slipped into a pattern of spending an afternoon with her once or twice a week and of occasionally giving her books or toys for the children. We worked together over a life history, kinship terminology and usage, children's stories, and the composition and activities of the various women's clubs of which she was a member and leader (one of which I joined). We occasionally digressed into more intellectual discussions when she asked me, in turn, about the Rosenberg case, America's H-bomb, and the position of women in America.

Another regular informant was a young man from an important Moslem family in town who came to our house at first ostensibly to help me improve my Javanese but soon simply to answer my questions about events in his own life and extensive family, in addition to relating a long series of dreams and doing projective tests. My relationship to him was very much one of an older sister with a younger brother. This informant I paid, as I did a third excellent one, a woman of my age with three children. This was the woman I call Juminah. She was a peddler in the market, selling cigarettes for tiny profits, and her husband was a poor carpenter. She was exceedingly talkative and unusually frank and concrete in her comments on her friends and relatives. Although I visited her from time to time in her own house, usually she came to mine, which meant that she did not have to be concerned about being overheard. Next to Bu Ardjo and my observations of the Ardjo family, Juminah was my best source on women's attitudes toward family relationships. My role with her was one of co-worker at a level of equality; and she felt that what she had to tell me was of interest and use to me. I could both take notes and use the dictaphone in her presence. She was without self-consciousness or pretense. She told me details of her life as a child in a nearby village, traditional religious customs, how to go about selling cigarettes and furniture, stories of her past and present experiences with family and friends, childbirth and child-care beliefs and practices, credit and pawning, town-based ritual cults, ideas on sex (one subject on which she was, like every other Javanese I met, very reticent), and household expenses.

I had five or six other informants of this caliber: a pious tailor's wife whose three daughters had grown up to become wives of rising young Moslem politicians, and whose family was infused with a new, rationalistic kind of piety; a more old fashioned pious Moslem woman who had been divorced and remarried twice and who was bringing up her four children on meager earnings by sewing for a local tailor; a wife of a policeman who had never lost her village ways when she moved into town with him, and who had her first child while I was there; a second (polygamous) wife of a leftist clerk in the Dutch hospital, who, trailed by her six-year-old son, was always busy organizing political meetings; a newly widowed wife of a high civil servant with seven young children; a young unmarried woman schoolteacher from an old Modjokuto family that had changed in three generations from wealthy farmers to well-off teachers and civil servants.

In addition to these informants with whom I worked intensively, seeing them between fifteen and forty times, there were about thirty more homes that I visited several times. To supplement my material, which was gathered mainly from women, I have drawn on my husband's notes on life histories of five Modjokuto men: two civil servants, a village religious official, and two pious Moslem traders, and on scattered notes from him on the family life of his other informants. All in all, some fifteen families were studied intensively; and thirty others were visited two times or more.

Table V

Social Position of Families Studied

| | INTENSIVELY STUDIED | | SOURCE OF ADDITIONAL INFORMATION | |
OCCUPATION	Low Income	Medium Income	Low Income	Medium Income
Office Workers	3	3	1	5
Teachers	—	2	—	4
Traders	3	—	6	5
Craftsmen	2	—	1	—
Laborers	1	—	6	—
Peasants	1	—	2	—
TOTALS	10	5	16	14

The problem of sampling is one which has plagued all anthropologists. Every descriptive statement includes a quantitative element, a suggestion that such-and-such a belief or behavior pattern is "typical" or "usual." This is especially a matter of concern in studying a complex society such as Java, where a long history, a dense population spread over a large area, and high social structural differentiation make for high variability on every dimension of analysis. The anthropologist must constantly ask himself, first, to what social group his generalization is referable, and, second, to what extent the generalization holds for all individuals within the group, or under what social conditions it is likely to be true.

Table VI

Religious Outlook of Families Studied

RELIGION	INTENSIVELY STUDIED	SOURCE OF ADDITIONAL INFORMATION
Abangan	4	11
Santri	6	10
Prijaji	5	9
TOTALS	15	30

Care was taken to make certain that the informants selected represent a wide range of social variation within the town, and as general regularities in family life appeared I constantly checked them for variations traceable to subgroup membership. I was under a disadvantage, at first, however, of not being sure just what the subgroups of Modjokuto were. Even the question of whether or not the town of Modjokuto was a significant social unit was in doubt during the first months of study. During the field work, the first main dimension of social differentiation taken most fully into account was that of class status, which is a complex product of economic differences, differences in occupational prestige, and certain intangible social evaluations of style of life and relative sophistication. The second was that of religio-ideological commitment, the distinction that is referred to in these pages as that between *abangan, santri,* and *prijaji*—Javanese animistic syncretism, puristic Islam, and Hindu-Buddhist mysticism. Subgroups according to these two dimensions—nearness to elite status, and religious variation—were the ones against which all generalizations were checked, and variations in these general statements have been reported where found.

INDEX